D0712717

# 80/20 Your Life:

*Get More Done With Less Effort, Time, and Action*

by Nick Trenton

www.NickTrenton.com

# Table of Contents

# Chapter 1. The World Turns 80/20

Imagine the following scenarios. You need to pick some clothes to wear at home from your wardrobe. Out of all the casualwear you own, how likely are you to choose that one favorite top or T-shirt you always wear despite having loads of other options? One theory suggests that you actually only wear the same few clothes in rotation, and your choice will likely be restricted to those clothes. You may not even consider any of the other options unless you're looking for a change. Yet those '80s band T-shirts and ripped sweatpants are still taking up room in your drawers, leaving your space crammed and disorganized.

Here's another one. Think of all the apps on your phone, and how many of them you actually use regularly. Maybe you're the kind of person who only keeps the most essential ones, but if you were to check your usage statistics, you'd probably discover you use the same few apps over and over, with the rest taking up only limited portions of your time. These other apps are using up valuable space in your phone, and may ultimately cause it to run out of storage or work less effectively if you don't take the time to clean them out.

Now think of all the creative ideas you've ever had when it comes to your work or studies. If you're an entrepreneur these ideas could be about what kind of business to start and how to grow or improve your existing one. If you're a writer these might concern the topics you think are worth writing about, and so on. In all honesty, how many of these ideas have been genuinely viable? It's probably only a minuscule percentage.

Let that sink in: *most* of the clothing in your wardrobe, the apps on your phone and the plans you spend your time daydreaming about don't actually end up being all that important. Rather, it's only the tiniest fraction of your ideas, items, actions, etc. that really matter.

What do all of these scenarios have in common? They suggest that in different areas of our lives, a small minority of things are the most important. Be it the technology we use, the objects we own or the ideas we have, the same few patterns repeat themselves again and again. We use the same apps, implement only a few of our ideas, and we generally wear the same handful of clothes from our wardrobe.

And yet, our wardrobes are still overflowing, our phones are crammed full of apps we don't use, and we're constantly told that all ideas are equally valuable. Not only do we make use of only a small amount of what we have, but we also tend to fill our lives with things that we can most likely do without. This emphasis on having and doing more pervades almost all areas of our lives, despite it not serving any meaningful purpose.

Without acknowledging this imbalance, we could waste time and energy on things in life that make no material difference to our success or happiness, all the while ignoring those aspects that have the real impact.

These aren't just casual observations. The phenomenon behind this human tendency has been thoroughly studied, so that we can make the most out of it in our professional and personal lives. Today, it's popularly known as the 80/20 principle. As we will see, cutting out the excess while focusing on the few things that do matter has several benefits. Not only does it save us time and resources, but it also rids us of the constant anxiety that comes with the pursuit of more.

This book explores the ins and outs of how the 80/20 principle manifests in our lives, how we can use it to our advantage, and the many ways in which it will improve your life for the better. Once you learn how to spot the 20% that matters, and let go of the 80% that doesn't, you'll discover an altogether new way of going about things that will be much more productive and conducive to success and well-being.

What is the 80/20 Principle?

**Briefly, according to the 80/20 principle, 20% of causes or inputs into any sort of endeavor result in 80% of the outcomes and results.**

This principle was first formulated by a renowned Italian economist named Vilfredo Pareto. This is why it's also known as the Pareto principle. Pareto first observed this 80/20 distribution in his homeland with respect to the wealth and population of Italy. He noticed that 80% of land in Italy was owned by only 20% of the population. Further research revealed that this is the case in several other countries, too.

Since then, the 80/20 distribution has been observed in a staggering array of fields unrelated to economics. The numbers don't necessarily have to be 80 and 20; these have just been chosen to indicate an uneven relationship between cause and effect. The rule could well be 95/5 instead of 80/20—it conveys the same message. Though there is no cosmic law stipulating that all things necessarily arrange themselves in such lopsided ratios, it does seem to be an uncannily common observation across various spheres of life. Our successes, failures, problems, and their solutions all seem to be in some way determined by how we use (or fail to use) the 80/20 principle.

For example, it's been found that 20% of our effort into projects results in 80% of our success. This runs contrary to the belief that the more effort we put into our endeavors, the more likely we are to be successful. It also explains those people who appear to be able to juggle multiple complicated tasks at the same time, and do all of it right with minimal effort. These are the people who know how to work in efficient and carefully planned ways. Familiarizing yourself with the Pareto principle can help you too become an overachiever who doesn't waste time on those things that are unlikely to move you forward.

A popular example of how the Pareto principle can help us get on top of problems comes from an anecdote involving Microsoft. They found that, by fixing the top 20% of the most common bugs in their software, they were able to eliminate 80% of the issues plaguing it. Out of these, 1% of the top 20% bugs caused half of all errors. "One really exciting thing we learned is how, among all these software bugs involved in the report, a relatively small proportion causes most of the errors," claimed Microsoft CEO Steve Ballmer. "About 20% of the bugs causes 80% of all errors, and—this is stunning to me—1 percent of bugs caused half of all errors."

Using this insight, Ballmer implemented a debugging procedure that saw Microsoft remove 20% total of all Windows XP bugs—a figure that would undoubtedly be lower if they had tackled the problem beginning with any of the less significant issues.

A caveat is that these bugs, though small in number, were actually among the most complex, and fixing them may well trigger new problems. Nevertheless, the key takeaway here is that fixing every aspect of a problem, in this case removing *all* the bugs from Windows, isn't necessarily the best way to go about things. Taking care of just a small, but the most important, part of an issue can produce returns that are worth many times the effort you put in.

A good way to summarize the Pareto principle is that life isn't fair. Things almost never work out in egalitarian ways. In an ideal world, every employee would contribute in similar ways to their organization, we'd be rewarded based on the quantity of our efforts, and things would generally have relatively the same value. But the truth is you don't get returns based on how much input you provide, the playing field across industries isn't level but dominated by a few elite performers, and most of what we spend our time on isn't valuable or productive.

At this point there might be a question on your mind. You may think that even though not all things provide equal value, surely they're all still important? The 20% you put into a project might get you 80% of the success you hoped for, but you still need to put in the remaining 80% of work because that is often the hardest. We don't usually just go 80% of the way in whatever we do, and to reach 100%, don't we inevitably have to put in the extra effort?

There is some truth to this claim, especially when it comes to acquiring new skills. Eighty percent of your proficiency in most things can be acquired by focusing on the most important 20%, but to be among the best, you'll need to go beyond that and master your art.

The point of the principle, however, is not to discount the importance of the 80% effort that only yields 20% returns. It's to emphasize the fact that just 20% of concentrated, smartly applied effort can give you as much as 80% of your desired outcome. What's important to learn is how to determine exactly which 20% needs the most attention, as well as how you can make any effort or input beyond that more efficient.

We've briefly mentioned the story of Pareto discovering the 80/20 principle through his economic research into property ownership across Italy and the world. However, there is much more to the history of this rule, with many besides Pareto playing a crucial role in theorizing and popularizing the principle.

Pareto was an extraordinary pioneer in business and economics, but alas, he was terrible at conveying his genius. Nobody before him had thought of taking two related sets of data, like distribution of property and the number of owners, and comparing percentages between them. Unfortunately, Pareto's later sociological work came to be hijacked by Mussolini and the Fascist party. This led to his 80/20 principle being ignored by academics for almost five decades, until it was rediscovered by two individuals in the aftermath of World War II.

The first of these individuals was a Harvard professor of philology named George Zipf. He called his version of the 80/20 rule the

"Principle of Least Effort." According to this principle, different resources like people, goods, time, skills, capital, and other productive assets tended to distribute themselves in ways that minimized the required work. So 20-30% of any resource accounted for 70-80% of whatever the resource was being used for.

For example, if you notice the words you use in routine conversation, you'll observe that you rarely use the full extent of your vocabulary. While speaking to others, we use approximately 20% of all words we know 80% of the time because it's one of the ways we make communication simpler. The speaker conserves energy by not having to think of too many elaborate words, while the listener doesn't have to expend too much brainpower in trying to understand what's being said.

At the heart of this principle is an assumption that humans tend to work in ways that allow them to apply the "least effort." An astonishing way in which Professor Zipf proved this is by going through all Philadelphia marriage licenses that were approved in a twenty-block radius. He was trying to see how far apart married couples initially lived from one another, and discovered that 70% of all couples married those who lived within 30% of a twenty-block area. Turns out, people don't venture too far from home in search of a life partner!

He also used this principle to explain why so many of us have messy desks. It's because the objects cluttering it are the ones we use frequently, and refraining from organizing the desk makes access to these items easier. This allows us to apply the least effort.

Besides Zipf, another person who formulated the 80/20 principle in slightly different terms was a Romanian-born US engineer named Joseph Moses Juran. Juran was interested in what factors went into improving the quality of components for different commodities like electronics and cars, and how manufacturing companies could boost the quality of their products with the least investment. In 1951 he published a book on this subject, which attracted the attention of the Japanese.

After World War II, Japan wanted to transition from being a military power to an economic one. However, their manufacturing sector had a well-established reputation for poor quality, and Juran was brought in to solve the problem. After two decades of work with several companies, Japan successfully shook off this reputation and became known as a world leader in terms of manufacturing quality.

At the same time, Juran's own country, the US, was going through a crisis of quality. Juran emphasized the role of a small number of defects causing the most problems, the few team members of a project that were bringing in most of its success, and the limited clientele that would give the Japanese most of their business. His success, while initially ignored, was quickly recognized in the US, where he was called back to replicate the results he managed to achieve in Japan.

After the quality revolution, technology giant IBM was one of the first corporations to use the 80/20 principle effectively. In 1963, IBM discovered that their computers spent 80% of their time trying to execute just 20% of their code. IBM took this 20% that was being used the most and made it more accessible and user-friendly, increasing the efficiency and speed of their important applications, and giving the company an edge over their competitors.

The 80/20 rule is so significant primarily because of our constant, if misguided, expectation of fair and equitable results from life. We tend to believe that doing good will result in the same amount of good coming back to us, that all our thoughts and musings are valuable, and that everyone is capable of providing the same value under ideal conditions.

We assume that our problems have causes that are all equally important for resolving them, that all the opportunities which come our way have the same potential for growth, and that there aren't just one or two relevant factors while the rest are relatively useless. Sometimes these expectations are justifiable, but generally this 50/50 way of thinking results in much misfortune.

The 80/20 principle does away with this misconception entirely. It suggests that if you properly analyze causes and effects, you'll inevitably conclude that some causes are much more important than others. The imbalance could be any conceivable ratio, be it 80/20, 90/10, 95/5, or even 99/1, but what remains constant is the lopsided contribution of some causes relative to others.

The two numbers needn't add up to a hundred, either. An axiom of the Pareto principle is that, whatever the level of imbalance, it's probably more pronounced than it seems at first. You might've known that you use some applications and features on your phone more than others, but have you ever thought of exactly how much you rely on those few apps? If you were to look closely, the true ratio would likely be steeper than you thought.

This phenomenon also shows that, despite how counterintuitive the principle is to our way of thinking, it does have real-world applications. Be it with your work, your social life, or your hobbies, the way you use your time and resources has a direct impact on the outcomes you achieve. By familiarizing yourself with the 80/20 principle, you can be happier and more at ease in your personal life and more successful in your professional one.

Using this principle, all you need to do is reorganize and reprioritize so you're being as efficient as possible, and the results will follow. Success also relies on substituting the unproductive elements or components with better ones, or simply eliminating them altogether.

Say you have ten hours to prepare for an exam. Eighty percent of your preparedness will be determined by how you spend approximately two of those ten hours. To maximize the efficiency of your study, you should start with these two hours of intense studying to get to know your subject matter instead of slacking off early and trying to recover later. Eliminate unproductive elements like distractions during those two hours, and spend the rest of the eight hours in ways that require less effort to achieve the remaining 20% of the preparation.

If you didn't know about the 80/20 rule, you might have tried spreading out your work in ways that would allow for its completion over ten hours. But with this rule, you could actually finish much earlier. While understanding the principle saves you time and enhances your productivity, it can also result in uncomfortable realizations.

To take another exampleL it's often observed that 20% of customers or products account for 80% of a company's profits. However, it's also true that 80% of what the company produces and 80% of their employees are not contributing proportionately. All that manpower and all those resources are effectively being wasted—and they might even be holding back the successful 20%.

The obvious question that arises is, why not just cut the unproductive 80% out? Companies refrain from asking uncomfortable questions like these, because the answers may mean they have to change four-fifths of what they're doing right now.

Similarly, once we realize that four-fifths of how we spend our time on important projects contributes close to nothing, it can be hard to accept the need for change. But while businesses can be extraordinarily slow at rearranging their resources and efforts, the process is much simpler for us as individuals. Finding and making the most of the "vital few" resources can multiply our results many times over despite putting in the "least effort." This is what makes the 80/20 principle so valuable: the promise of exponential growth.

## The 80/20 Principle and How the World Turns

As we've discussed, the Pareto principle can be applied to almost any area of life. Everywhere you look, you can probably spot inefficiencies and resources that aren't being used in the best way possible. Either that, or some outcomes are disproportionately being caused by small groups of people or factors. Here are a few examples:

- 80% of box office revenue is generated by 1-2% of all films
- 80% of a person's happiness and achievements are experienced in 20% of their life
- Half of all guns in the US belong to 3% of the population
- 80% of all flowers grow as a result of 20% of planted seeds
- 80% of sales derive from 20% of the advertising that a company invests in
- 80% of all shared social media posts are from 20% of updates
- 20% of the exercises you do during a workout creates 80% of the results
- 20% of what your teacher tells you creates 80% of your total understanding of the topic
- Cleaning 20% of a room seems to account for 80% of its perceived tidiness

- 20% of your experiences will make up 80% of your most cherished memories
- 20% of your financial decisions are 80% responsible for your current financial state
- 20% of your good habits result in 80% of the total positive outcome from all of them

Though the internet is filled with similar statistics that aren't backed up by any research or data, the prevalence of lopsided relations between inputs and outputs is nonetheless very high. These statistics are also generally focused on business; however, there are many surprising areas where this phenomenon can be observed.

One such example is in the alcohol industry. A study found that people who consume wine, beer, and spirits account for approximately 80% of all sales involving these three types of alcohol (Habel, et al 2003). This has helped alcohol companies to more effectively market their products. It also helps them decide whether they should increase their brand penetration, attempt to cultivate more loyalty among existing users, or encourage more frequent purchase.

This is a classic example of the Pareto principle being used in the context of business. Other ways this rule manifests itself in business:

- 20% of all customers make up 80% of all complaints a company receives
- 80% of a company's profit comes from 20% of its efforts
- 20% of employees account for 80% of all sales

It's this 20% that businesses need to focus on to maximize their profits and unlock long-term growth.

Besides commercial enterprises, sports is another sphere where the Pareto principle can be observed. It's thought that 20% of players on a team are responsible for 80% of its success. For sports like soccer and cricket, this means that just two out of every eleven are doing the heavy lifting for the squad.

However, the phenomenon varies in proportion across different sports. For example, it's more prevalent in basketball than in a sport like ice hockey—80% of all points scored in basketball are attributed to 20% of the top-earning players, whereas in hockey, the distribution is much more even (Perry 2008).

Another unexpected area where this principle applies is online dating. If you've spent any time on dating apps like Tinder, this might not surprise you. Recent reports have suggested that the 80% of men with the least likes on Tinder are competing for the bottom 22% of women in terms of likes. Conversely, 78% of women with the most likes are competing for the 20% men that have received the most attention. One reason that explains this distribution is that women form only a small minority of all people on Tinder (22%). However, in another way, this further exacerbates the imbalance wherein large numbers of men can choose between the bottom fifth of these 22% women, while the other four-fifths have a much larger population of men to choose from (Iqbal 2020).

Next, we have healthcare services. The Department of Health and Human Services released a report in 2012 which stated that 5% of the population consumes 50% of US healthcare expenditures. The study also relies on earlier data, showing that this distribution had existed for at least five years before the study was published.

Lastly, the 80/20 rule has been observed in academia, and the results can be quite serious (Nelson, 2015). Some reports suggest that 90% of all academic papers in the humanities go uncited. This means that only 10% of all published papers are ever cited, which is a disheartening statistic for budding researchers.

Different studies have yielded different figures. One pegs the imbalance at an 80/20 distribution, while others are more generous in their claims that it's closer to a 65/35 ratio. However, we can't avoid the evidence that most academic papers are simply never used productively once they're published, and only a small percentage receive widespread attention.

As you can see, the Pareto principle is everywhere—even where you don't expect it. Given how often huge multinational companies use the Pareto rule to make their business models more efficient, there's every reason to believe that you can do the same with your personal life as well. The mechanism remains the same; only the context changes. All you need to do is spot the 20% of your life that is having the biggest impact, and the 80% deadweight that is taking up too much of your time and resources. The next chapter tells you how to do exactly this.

Takeaways

- According to the 80/20 principle, there are a small set of inputs or factors that make the biggest impact on the total outcome. Roughly 20% of the effort is behind 80% of the results. The numbers can vary widely, with 80 and 20 being just one distribution, and this pattern is observed not just in the business world, but in our personal lives as well.

- This rule was first discovered by the Italian economist Vilfredo Pareto. While observing the distribution of property amongst the Italian population, he found that 20% of Italians own 80% of all private property. He researched this phenomenon further and discovered that this lopsided distribution is prevalent in many other countries as well. Unfortunately, Pareto's ground-breaking discovery was ignored for several decades before others independently observed the same patterns.

- Once the principle was rediscovered, it was adopted by large tech companies like IBM, which used it to improve their computer software. This and similar successes led to the principle's popularization.

- One of the main reasons the 80/20 rule is so important is that it goes against our conventional way of thinking. We tend to assume that the world is a fair place, that things always work out in egalitarian ways, and that one factor is generally as valuable as the next. However, the Pareto principle reverses this belief by saying that only a few elements are truly worth our effort.

- You can see the Pareto principle everywhere around you. Be it dating apps, where large numbers of men are chasing very few women, or sports, where a couple of players determine the team's success, a few causes dominate the end results. By tapping into this potential of the vital few in your own life, you can use the Pareto principle to great effect.

To use the principle in your academic studies, identify only those chapters, concepts, or definitions that help you understand the bulk of the material—e.g. study just the key chemical equations in a chapter first, and spend less effort going over the examples and illustrations.

In your personal life, zoom in on only those activities that most constitute "quality time" with your partner, and always prioritize those. At work, regularly ask what's actually effective and deliberately spend less time doing things like admin or useless process work. The principle even applies when you focus on the only piece of constructive/negative feedback you've received. Using this to inspire your improvements will be so much more effective than considering dozens of complimentary but vague comments.

# Chapter 2. The 80/20 Rule as a Life Principle

So far, we've looked at many examples of the Pareto principle in the world around us. Once you start to look for it, you may see it everywhere. But the point is not just to observe the principle in effect, but to find ways we can actively use this insight to improve our own lives.

Doing so might be challenging at first, primarily because it may require you to reorient and modify the way you approach different situations, tasks, and problems. Old habits die hard, but if we wish to optimize our personal lives, this is a small sacrifice in the interest of self-improvement and exponential growth. You can start doing this today by understanding three simple rules: *less is more, always work backwards,* and *most things don't matter.*

The first step toward reorienting your life to fully exploit the 80/20 rule is to try and understand that **less is more**. We are constantly told that we must do more and more to achieve good results. This is often because we aren't confident in our abilities to perform the essentials of what is required in various situations. In life there is so much we can't control, but we can counter this somewhat by throwing everything we can at a problem, pulling out all the stops and ramping up the effort.

The underlying (but incorrect) assumption is that effort is proportional to outcome, so if we're unsure about what to do next, we may just double down on what we're doing instead of pausing to consider whether we should be doing it at all.

As a result, we fill our schedules to the brim so they're packed for weeks and months on end. After all, everyone else seems to be doing the same thing. Regardless of whether this strategy actually works for us, it *feels* like it does. By putting in massive amounts of (not necessarily productive) effort, we can assure ourselves, "at least I put in the work!" even if it didn't get us the results we wanted.

But it's perfectly possible to "work hard," to put in the hours and to slog away, but come up with no real result at the end of it all. Being your own slave driver will not necessarily win you any prizes—it's more a question of the *efficiency and appropriateness* of your efforts, rather than their raw intensity.

This need to overcompensate and do as much as we possibly can has two major downsides. Firstly, there are negative implications for our well-being. As we struggle to juggle the many obligations we've filled our calendars with, we tend to prioritize them over everything that is dear to us. Be it our physical and mental health, social lives, families, interests, or leisure time, all of it ceases to matter when we pressure ourselves into believing that more work is the only way to be successful.

The other downside is that we make all these sacrifices for returns that are usually not worthwhile, and could have been achieved with much less effort anyway. More often than not, we do this simply to ensure that we don't regret not trying harder, and to avoid dealing with the uneasiness that comes with feeling like you should be doing more. However, once you learn to use the 80/20 principle effectively, the positive results you experience will help you cope with these doubts and fears because you'll have seen firsthand that less can indeed be more.

Our second rule is to **work backwards**. Knowing your end goal will make applying the 80/20 rule in your personal life significantly easier. The lack of a defined goal inevitably means that we spend our time on tasks that *seem* related to our ultimate objective, but are often not, or are only loosely connected. If you understand your goal clearly, you're more likely to understand exactly what impacts the goal— and what doesn't.

When you identify a clear, direct line between your efforts now and how they bring your goal to life, you can tune out the noise and distraction along the way. If you don't have a goal in clear focus, you risk getting bogged down in irrelevant details that do nothing to bring you closer to your desired end.

If your goal is a fuzzy "be healthier" then you may waste time buying useless exercise gear or gimmicky diet supplements, or spend ages planning out a new workout routine that ultimately has no chance of giving you the results you are after—and how could it, when you're not even sure yourself of the results you're after? You end up getting tangled in details while the goal remains unrealized.

These details are often the small filler tasks we choose to do first instead of the harder ones. Completing them might feel like you're slowly but steadily making progress toward your goal, but as the old adage goes, no pain no gain. If it feels easy, it probably isn't providing you with much return on your efforts.

For example, let's say you've decided to start eating healthy. You ditch all the junk food for veggies, fruits, and salads. But what is the ultimate goal here? Are you trying to lose weight or gain muscle? Depending on your answer, what you need to eat can change substantially. If you don't start out with a clear goal, you might deprive yourself of your favorite foods without making any progress toward your goal. On the other hand, with a crystal-clear end goal, you could decide on an appropriate diet much sooner, and consequently see results faster.

To aid you in the process of zeroing in on your ultimate goal, make a list of all the tasks you need to do in a given situation. Flag the ones that are most important to the completion of your project, and tackle those first.

The last step is to realize that **most things don't matter**. Another way you'll want to modify your approach to make better use of the 80/20 principle is to first ask yourself plenty of questions depending on the situation you find yourself in.

Say you find yourself navigating a rough patch in your relationship. Ask yourself things like, "What are two or three of the biggest issues plaguing my relationship?", or "What is the one thing I can improve about myself to ameliorate these issues?" Notice that both of these questions focus on the *biggest* factors relating to your issues with your partner, but not *all* factors.

Answer these questions honestly, and then start doing the things you need to do. So, if you think you could be more open and forthcoming with your partner, make an active effort to do so. Of course, this is easier said than done.

Often, the biggest tasks and problems make us the most anxious. This makes us run away and avoid them while we turn our focus toward smaller problems that seem more manageable. We enjoy the illusion of making progress when in reality, the problem is unsolved, or even worsened. This is the second step that accompanies asking yourself tough questions—and following through on the tough answers they come with.

Here's another example of how to perform this two-step technique. Let's assume you want to build your muscle mass and improve your fitness levels. Ask yourself questions like these:

What are the two most beneficial habits I can adopt that will have the biggest long-term impact on my fitness?
What are two or three of the worst habits that I need to eliminate to become a healthy individual?
What are the biggest lifestyle barriers preventing me from maintaining a healthy routine?

Some common answers to these questions might be drinking more water, tracking your calories, and cutting down on smoking, drinking and junk food, or long working hours, respectively. While all of this might sound like a tall order, incorporating these changes into your lifestyle is incomparably easier than slogging it out tirelessly at a gym without having these habits in place. As such, you can make a few daunting but effective lifestyle changes instead of simply hitting the gym day in and day out without seeing the results that depend on these essential habits.

A similar approach can be followed in any area of your life. If you're looking for an example set of questions to ruminate over, here are some suggestions to get you started:

- What are the biggest distractions that disrupt my workflow?
- What are the best ways I can cut down on major expenses to save more money?
- Which possessions of mine are the most expendable?
- Which activities do I enjoy least and can be eliminated from my routine?
- Who are the people in my life that bring me the most joy and stability?
- What are the biggest stressors in my life and what can I do about them?

- What are the best habits I can incorporate which have the most net positive effect on my life (reading, healthier eating, etc.)?

Once you've carried out these three steps a few times and gained some practice, you're likely to notice a shift in your mindset and approach toward daily life and goals. You'll experience a heightened clarity and sense of purpose or focus. Changing the way you think will remain a process that takes time, but any progress in that direction will prepare you for the next steps toward implementing the 80/20 principle in your life more holistically.

A Word of Caution

This is where we discuss the potential dangers, and the ways the 80/20 rule might be used incorrectly. Some of these mistakes have already been discussed briefly, but we'll go into greater depth here. There are several common misconceptions surrounding the Pareto principle—let's consider each of them.

## Misconception 1: The numbers always need to be 80 and 20

This is the most obvious assumption because these numbers are stated in the rule itself, so it's natural to use them as guidelines in your applications. Furthermore, most criticisms of the Pareto principle are based on this misconception.

It's argued that those numbers only apply to a limited number of scenarios, but there's actually no rule about a rigid ratio of 80 to 20. The main relevance of using these two numbers is to illustrate the lopsided relationship between input and output. The ratio can be 99/1, 70/5, 82/10, and so on.

Later in the book we'll look at how this principle can apply to more abstract concepts like relationships or general well-being and happiness, which are naturally impossible to quantify. This is why it's important to realize that the numbers in the 80/20 rule are purely illustrative, and meant to convey an unbalanced relationship, however we quantify it—or even whether we quantify it or not.

## Misconception 2: The numbers need to add up to 100

The fact that the numbers add up to 100 is only because that's the original distribution Pareto discovered in Italy regarding its population and land ownership. In truth, the numbers could add up to any number greater or less than 100. This is because there will be many aspects in a situation that simply don't contribute anything, or are neutral.

So if you have to do ten tasks, don't automatically assume that around two of them are the most important. Instead, use your judgement to gauge which of the tasks are most significant and spend the bulk of your energy on them.

## Misconception 3: The 80/20 rule encourages laziness

Given the constant emphasis on doing less rather than more, it's easy to think that the

Pareto principle condones doing only the least amount of work, i.e. that it's great for the laziest among us. But nothing could be further from the truth. To truly understand this principle, we need to completely shift our understanding of what doing "less" means.

What counts is results and outcomes. If you expend less energy achieving the same result as someone else who spends more energy achieving the same thing, then it's not that you've done "less" or they've done "more"—rather, one path was more elegant, direct and efficient than the other.

The insistence on doing less is inseparable from the focus on being efficient and productive. This requires careful planning, cultivating good judgment, and staying disciplined. Laziness will almost certainly guarantee failure.

Misconception 4: The 80% can be ignored entirely

This misconception is probably a result of the Pareto principle's glorification of the

20% that's most important across different scenarios, but this does not mean that the remaining 80% can simply be ignored. After all, nobody can consistently ignore less important aspects of life—presidents still have to brush their teeth, top athletes still have to file tax returns.

The idea is just to spend the least amount of time possible on these less crucial aspects while prioritizing the 20%. Even if you choose to delegate 80% of your work that you deem comparatively unimportant, you'll still need to track and manage it to ensure that that part is being carried out appropriately as well. Yes, it's not your priority, but it doesn't mean you can completely ignore it.

Now that you know which misconceptions to avoid, we'll discuss the role of judgment in using the Pareto principle effectively. You may have wondered, in reading the previous sections, about an obvious weakness to the principle in general: how can we ever be sure we are correctly identifying what is the most important aspect in any endeavor?

Whenever perceptions and judgements are involved, mistakes are inevitable, especially in the beginning. This is not a weakness in the model per se, but simply an unavoidable consequence of us being flawed human beings who often work with incomplete knowledge.

When you're using the Pareto principle for your business, the role of judgment is minimized because you have data to help you make decisions. However, when it comes to your personal life, we are bound to prioritize the wrong factors and mistakenly group them into the most important 20%. It takes practice and observation to get better at this.

Thankfully, it isn't too difficult to gauge how much of a difference specific activities and inputs make to your final result. In addition, you can observe other people, how they go about doing things and what mistakes they make, and learn from them.

In personal matters, it's natural to freeze up and become anxious of making the wrong judgments. This can only be countered by a genuine commitment toward refining our judgment and prioritizing results over what feels right in the short term.

There are also ways to go about using the 80/20 principle in our personal lives in a more data-oriented manner. Use a diary or journal to keep track of your progress based on the decisions you take, and analyze the results from time to time. Give yourself time to collect enough data and information—one or two months at the most and a week at the least—and base your judgements on what you've collected.

Perhaps the biggest reason we're constantly tempted to do more instead of less is our quest for perfection. We want to be able to control and improve every single facet of the situation we find ourselves in, even if that means dedicating excessive resources and time to these endeavors. However, even if we choose to adopt the 80/20 principle, it's still easy to transfer our perfectionism to the 20% we feel is most important. We have less to agonize over, but still enough to overwork ourselves in ways that are not necessarily conducive to achieving results.

One of the most important parts about learning to incorporate the 80/20 principle in your life is to learn how to let go. To a large extent, this also applies to the 80% you've deemed less important. If you've delegated it, yet continue to micromanage that part of your work, you haven't really let go. Similarly, with the 20% that's important, you must know when to stop and recognize that you've done enough.

Here's an example. You're studying for a test that's based on one book you've been assigned for the course. Out of the chapters in this book, you've identified three that are most important, and your knowledge of these sections guarantees you'll pass the test. The perfectionist in us might be tempted to review these three chapters endlessly. But this would defeat the purpose of adopting the Pareto principle because you likely won't end up reducing your overall workload.

Instead, set out a time period that you think will be sufficient to gain a good grasp of those three chapters, and let it go after that. This will not only ensure better retention, but also help you implement the 80/20 rule more effectively in the future because of the better results it will yield you.

Illustrating the 80/20 Rule

When used correctly, the Pareto principle can lead to great results through minimal effort. However, not every situation calls for the same approach. If you aren't careful about how you use the 80/20 rule, you may unwittingly suffer some negative consequences. Thankfully, it isn't difficult to recognize the kinds of situations that are appropriate for the Pareto principle and those that aren't.

One area where the Pareto principle can unquestioningly be applied in several productive ways is your career or business. This is the main reason behind the popularity of the rule in the first place!

When it comes to careers, arguably the best way to use the Pareto principle is to streamline your job search. Hunting for jobs involves researching, networking, and applying. All of these can take a lot of your time, but it doesn't necessarily have to be that way. Instead, divide your time over these three activities in efficient ways. Don't just apply to every job opportunity that comes your way, and, as tempting as it is, don't rely entirely on networking and contacts to get you a good job. Even within these three overarching activities related to your job search, some are worth it, while others aren't.

For example, researching prospective employers is a rabbit hole that's easy to fall into, and hard to get out of because of how important it seems. You might find job opportunities that appear interesting, but they're located in places you wouldn't want to move or commute to. Yet, you might be tempted to apply to these jobs as a backup in case nothing else works out.

Here, apply the Pareto Principle by identifying your geographical preferences for jobs early on, and searching for employees only in those regions. Give some thought to where you'd prefer working, and then find jobs available there. Since only a small number of positions is likely to be appropriate, narrow in on those soon in your search process, and save yourself the effort of considering loads of unsuitable positions. This way, you cut out the 80% wasted time spent looking for and applying for jobs you're unlikely to really want.

Another common tendency is to apply to jobs that don't quite fit your background or experience. Though this might give you more varied opportunities, it isn't always a good strategy. Starting out, only apply to jobs for which you fulfill 70% or more of the listed parameters. This will not only save you time that could be better spent elsewhere, but also the disappointment that comes with not hearing back.

You're much more likely to be rejected for jobs whose requirements you don't meet. Avoid applying to these and you'll save time and effort. The principle here is simple: only a tiny fraction of jobs is likely to be right for you, so focus on honing in on those positions.

If you work hard to pursue only the most eligible and appropriate 20% of jobs, you'll be more successful in your job search than if your technique was more scattershot. You may ultimately expend less energy, but the effort, being more targeted, is more effective. When combined with the previous tip, this will narrow down your search drastically while also providing you with the best options that suit your experience, background, and geographical preferences.

A third highly recommended strategy for getting jobs is to build your profile on social networking sites. Taking time to enhance your profile, expand your list of contacts, and enlarge your database can open new doors—but not all techniques are equal. Twenty percent of what you do on social networks will give you 80% of your returns.

Reaching out to a single key person who has the power to influence your career is more effective than constantly engaging hundreds of people who will never realistically improve your prospects. This will depend on your business or your skillset, but it would be foolish to think that pointless Facebook posting could yield the same results as a targeted, informed networking campaign on LinkedIn, for example.

In your career, once you're hired, the 80/20 rule can help you think carefully about what actions genuinely bring you closer to your goals. For example, in a dispute, it may make more sense for you to try to contact someone more senior from the get-go, or you may quickly discover that you've got more of a chance of getting what you want if you reach out to ten more junior people first. By constantly asking how your efforts and rewards weigh up, what you can ditch, and what you can focus on, you keep your eye on what matters and avoid getting bogged down by what doesn't.

These are just some of the ways you can implement the 80/20 rule in both your job search and your job itself. The trick is to work smart, not hard. Eliminate tasks that provide too little return for too much effort, and don't put all your eggs into one basket.

The beauty of this principle is that it lets you shape your approach to prioritize the people, products, and resources that offer the most value to your company. For example, let's say you're a restaurant owner. You've observed that around 80% of your revenue in a day is earned in 20% of your working hours. The peak time for your business is around eight to ten p.m., right when you usually shut your doors for the day. An effective way to use the principle here would be to extend your working hours by an hour at night while opening a few hours later in the morning to capitalize on peak hours.

A good way to break down the ways in which you can apply the 80/20 principle to your business is to split it into three major factors: *products, customers, and marketing.* Each of these likely takes up an overwhelming portion of your time and resources, so you'll want to make sure that they're always being optimized.

Regarding products, we know that 20% of products generate 80% of revenue. But how do you find out *which* 20%? For online stores, you can use tools like Google Analytics to track sales, whereas other software is available for brick-and-mortar stores.

Another way to narrow down products is to analyze the percentage of sales versus the percentage of profits. This is especially useful when some of your products require more customer support than others. Make a table and account for all related costs to your products and find out which ones are the most profitable and in demand with your customers. These are the ones you should advertise the most.

When it comes to customers, use a similar strategy. Find the 20% that are generating 80% of your revenue and regularly follow up with them and offer incentives to ensure they remain loyal. Additionally, find out which 20% are the cause of 80% of the complaints you receive, and consider how to convert them to happy clients, or eliminate them altogether, if possible.

Lastly, marketing your product will require the use of the Pareto principle in several domains. These include the way you manage search engine optimization, content marketing, social media outreach, web traffic, etc.

Using the 80/20 rule here has a lot to do with tracking relevant data for all of these categories, choosing the ones that generate the most leads, and capitalizing on them. You want to find the keywords, content, social media posts and so on that do the most work, and focus your efforts there. Can you cut what is underperforming or even hurting your ratings? Tools like Google Analytics help enormously with this, so spend some time familiarizing yourself with the program to boost sales and reduce inputs over the long-term.

When you use one tool for various activities relevant to your business, you'll save time that would otherwise be spent learning how to use different tools for different tasks. This might tempt you to just delegate this work, which means you'll expend resources on something you could easily do yourself. Instead, pick up a book or course on this topic, and you'll save yourself a lot of time and money in the long run.

Takeaways

- Three simple maxims can help us use the 80/20 rule in everyday life: *less is more, always work backwards, and most things don't matter*. Firstly, don't do a lot of busy work simply because it feels like you're making progress—always try to work smarter, not harder simply for the sake of working harder. Secondly, always make sure your goals are crystal clear so you can work backwards and decide which actions matter—and which don't. Finally, understand that some factors simply matter much less than others, and let go of the minor details to focus on the more important ones.
- Use smart questions to zoom in what ultimately matters. Get curious about the *biggest* rewards, costs, obstacles

and sources of joy, and don't worry about considering *all* of them.

- The numbers don't have to be in an 80/20 ratio and they don't need to add up to 100. Rather, the 80/20 fraction is simply meant to illustrate that one side of the equation is significantly larger than the opposite.

- Understand that the principle doesn't encourage laziness but optimizes the energy that you do spend, maximizing on its returns. At the same time, don't think that you can completely ignore the 80%--it needs your attention, just relatively less compared to the 20%.

- The effectiveness of the principle depends on your accuracy in identifying the most important 20%. You'll make mistakes in the beginning, but it's a learning curve— constantly check in with your appraisal and adjust as necessary. Gather objective data to analyze so you can make objective, rational decisions as much as possible.

- You can use the Pareto principle in your career, specifically your job search. Expend the least energy for the most reward by honing in on only those job roles most appropriate for you early on. This means you search less, and come up with fewer hits— but those hits will be of greater quality, saving you time and energy.
- You can use the Pareto principle in your business, too, by letting it guide your marketing efforts. Using gathered analytics data, for instance, you can identify the top performing posts, campaigns or keywords, so you can focus on those.

Though it's true that the principle isn't a magic formula that will solve all your problems (or save you from having to consider the 80%), it can be an enormous time and energy saver if used correctly. In short, the 80/20 principle is about using data or observations to help identify and optimize on the most essential aspects of any process, so that you spend the least energy for the most gain. A simple example is a company offering free samples at a convention. Using data, they can identify their top performing and most popular item and promote that exclusively, knowing that this move is likely to generate more revenue than any other.

# Chapter 3. The Less is More Framework

In the previous chapter we discussed some examples of how the 80/20 rule can be incorporated into your life. However, in this chapter, we'll give you a more robust framework for getting into the 80/20 mindset, examining various areas of your life using the Pareto principle, and assessing how this rule can be incorporated for maximum success. The tools and techniques described here will also help you dodge any potential misapplications of the principle. This will ensure that your productivity improves, you have more time to spend on leisure, and you aren't wasting effort in places that don't need it.

The Three-Step Framework

Richard Koch, author of *The 80/20 Principle* and perhaps the biggest proponent of this rule, recommends three simple steps to help you go about applying the 80/20 principle in various areas of your life.

Step 1 is to **identify your 80/20 goals**. We tend to have lots of goals, far too many to focus on simultaneously. The trouble is, not all goals are created equally. It's not uncommon to *think* you really want something, only to realize after you've started on it (or even actually achieved it) that it's not really what you want at all. The principle can help here: imagine that of all your goals, only a minority are going to supply the most satisfaction and achievement.

We seldom think to rank goals, and simply assume that achieving one will bring as much happiness as reaching the other. All of us would love to get in shape, make more money, go on a dream holiday, meet our soul mates and get our houses organized, but we have to be honest and identify those one or two goals that really cut to the heart of what matters to us in life—and this is invariably just one or two things.

Out of our multiple goals, we need to list out the 20% that are going to lead to the most happiness when we achieve them. Of course, all your goals are probably important to you, but a good way to separate the most crucial from the rest is to ask yourself which ones are more immediately significant. Say you have to choose between eating healthier and reading more. Which one can you wait to achieve, and which one would be more beneficial long-term if you started doing it today?

Another factor that can help you choose your goals is to consider whether they help you further your purpose in life. There's a good chance you might not know what that is yet, and you might not even believe in the concept of a life purpose. Regardless, you can still make use of this general guideline. It has been prescribed by many proponents of the Pareto principle, and here's how you can get closer to finding yours.

Chances are, you'll recognize tasks that bring you closer to your purpose instantly. These are the kind that you actually want to do and are passionate about. They bring out the perfectionist within you, and you won't need to push yourself to complete them. Tasks you enjoy are significantly more productive than ones you don't, and this is why finding goals aligning with your purpose is so important. You'll naturally finish these activities quickly and do them well without putting in too much effort, all while you enjoy yourself.

Out of all the goals you have, it's advisable to start with as few as possible so that you aren't stretching yourself too thin. Two to three is a good number, and make sure you start with the ones that need the most effort and change on your part. It's easy to put off these hard goals for later, but ultimately, you'll end up never achieving them.

The thing about these kinds of goals is that they also tend to be those that, once achieved, make the most material difference to your life. Many people, for example, spend time and effort in the gym to improve their health and appearance, while not significantly changing their poor eating habits, or quitting smoking or excessive drinking. Though both goals are important, the truth is that a better diet and quitting addictive behaviors is the more difficult goal—but also the one more likely to have an impact on your health and appearance.

Choosing the most difficult goal means you are selecting those results and outcomes that are likely to be most drastic, i.e. "big monsters, big prizes."

The next step is **identifying your 80/20 path**. For every goal you want to achieve, there are four possible paths to choose from when deciding how exactly to go about achieving them. These are: a) Low Effort, Low Reward, b) High Effort, Low Reward, c) High Effort, High reward, d) Low effort, High Reward.

You need to choose one of these paths and stick to it. Which one do you select? If your answer was the low effort, high reward path, you choose correctly. This is the path Koch calls the 80/20 path, and it is the simplest way to achieve the maximum results you're looking for.

Let's consider an example. Say you've taken a challenging course at college and want to get a good grade on it. This is your 80/20 goal. How would you go about charting an 80/20 path for it? If you went with the low effort, low reward route, you could just study on the days before examinations, bunk all your lectures, and wing the paper. You might manage to pass the course, but you'd likely only scrape through.

Maybe you took the high effort, low reward path. This is easily the worst one, and we tend to follow it more often than we realize. For our example, this would entail attending all your lectures but not paying attention, participating in class without being prepared, and making elaborate plans to study which you never follow through on. It's easy to see why you'd be better off not bothering with these efforts altogether.

The other very common path we generally choose is high effort, high reward. We do everything we possibly can to achieve our goals, and if we succeed it reinforces the belief that such extreme effort is the only way you can do well in life. So, if you attend all your lectures and participate diligently, complete all your homework, study and revise your materials daily, etc., all of this might ensure success, but at what cost? It will likely take up all of your time, make you skip meals and sleep, worry excessively, and generally harm your health.

Lastly, we have the low effort, high reward path. This would mean attending lectures where you know key concepts are going to be discussed. You'd do all the important assignments while delegating the ones that are strenuous but don't carry too much relevance for your grade. Further, you'd identify questions that are likely to appear in your exam either by yourself or with the help of classmates. You might also use powerful tools like mind maps to help you absorb information better. All of these ensure that you're making the most judicious use of your time while receiving the most return on your investment. This is clearly where we want to be strategizing toward.

Such paths can be formulated for every single goal you want to achieve, and charting them out beforehand can help tremendously. Here, one major issue you might face is regarding how to map out the low effort, high reward path. If you're struggling, try doing some research on the techniques and methods others have found useful in similar situations. Pick and choose the ones that appear most applicable and follow them appropriately. If you have people you can reach out to, don't hesitate and try to learn from them as well. Finally, take your own thoughts into account and chart the best 80/20 path.

The third and final step is **identifying your 80/20 actions**. When you're charting your 80/20 path, there are bound to be a few actions you take within that which will contribute inordinately to your end goal. We'll call these your 80/20 actions, and it's imperative that you identify these early on to make the most of them. As in creating the path itself, a useful guideline for identifying 80/20 actions is to observe what's worked for others. However, it is equally important to contrast that with what works for you.

Too often we look at successful people and try to copy what they did, only to realize that their solutions and tricks don't work for us. For example, the fact that most successful people wake up early doesn't mean that doing the same is going to be equally productive for you. Similarly, take advice from others, but consider for yourself how relevant the advice is for you. This might require some trial and error initially, so make sure you give yourself time to experiment.

It's important to not get too attached to any one approach or technique—it's the results that matter. You need to be able to appraise your results as you go and quickly adjust according to what works—and this holds true whether your actions match conventional wisdom or not. A little self-compassion and forgiveness goes a long way. If something doesn't quite work, see it as a useful data point and carry on with something different; you only waste time when you beat yourself up.

Over time, try and narrow down which of your actions will guarantee success when you perform them. For example, if you're a content creator and know that a certain keyword drives a lot of traffic to your website, don't waste time with the other less productive keywords. Create content based on what you know for a fact will work and generate positive results. Similarly, if you know that you're more productive during evenings than mornings, try and dedicate as much of your evenings to work as possible and reserve mornings for sleep, exercise, or other tasks.

To continue the example of wanting to score a good grade, your specific 80/20 actions will inevitably be subjective. Perhaps you can get by with just attending the lectures, or you might be the type who prefers to learn by yourself, in which case you can skip the lectures. Maybe you prefer studying for short periods regularly, or you might like studying for long stretches right before exams. Either way, identify the techniques that are most productive for you, and eliminate the rest.

Now that you've familiarized yourself with the theoretical aspect of applying the 80/20 rule, its time to see how these steps look in action. We've provided you with a basic framework for going about studying for a hard course, and below are two more examples of how to use these three steps.

Say your goal is to become physically fit. Your first step is to identify the important 80/20 goals that will contribute most toward you gaining muscle mass. Remember that you only need two to three. One of these will undoubtedly be your diet, so one of your 80/20 goals is to find ways to eat healthier because this will have the biggest impact on your gains. The second most important goal here is to work out vigorously at the gym. Going easy on your body has never produced results, and you need to push your limits to get the body you desire.

There are many miscellaneous goals we could've considered in addition to these, such as drinking more water, refraining from consuming alcohol, etc., but we've found the two goals that will have the most impact on your end result and we're going to stick to those.

Next, we identify our low effort, high reward path and apply it to both of our main goals. For working out, the way to apply it would be to do fewer, but tougher full-body exercises at the gym rather than spending hours busting it out with weights. This will save you time and effort in the long run, even though the short period of exercise itself will be demanding.

When it comes to eating healthy, think of all the healthy things you already like eating. Maybe you love bananas, great! Snack on bananas whenever possible. Maybe you prefer certain meats over others; consume more of those and try looking for some simple recipes to prevent your meals from becoming repetitive. This way, you're not spending energy adapting to a diet that doesn't accommodate your eating preferences. You're working with what you like and making the most of it.

Lastly, you need to identify your 80/20 actions. One way to do this is to determine which specific exercises are giving you the best results. You can do this by experimenting with your workouts and observing which seem to work better for you. If you follow one routine one week and another for a different week, one is bound to give you stronger fitness gains.

For your meals, identify foods that keep you full, but contain the least calories and most protein. Eating these foods is guaranteed to help you gain more muscle, and if they're things you already like eating, you'll have no difficulty consuming them regularly.

Let's consider another example, this time about inculcating good habits. Say your 80/20 goal is to read more. What's the path to reading more that involves the least effort and the highest reward? There are a few ways you can go about this.

One way is to simply visit the nearest library and scan through books till you find something you like. But this would be a massive waste of time. Ideally, you'll want to know what type of books you like to read before picking one up. A good place to start here is to think about which subjects you liked most in school. If it was science, you could give science fiction a try. If it was history, perhaps some historical fiction. If it was literature, then some classics might be enjoyable. The trick here is to go with what is familiar and appealing to you. For our purpose, let's assume you've decided to go with classics.

Now you need to find a book to read. Again, you won't want to spend too much time scrolling through endless options. Every genre has its top picks, and their popularity makes it likely that you'll find them exciting as well. Since you're just starting out, you'll also want a short book to see if you actually like the genre.

As such, Fitzgerald or Hemingway would make for a good first choice. Now you need to set up a reading routine. The secret to inculcating new habits is doing something consistently for extended periods of time, and reading is no different. Read every day for thirty minutes to an hour, and you should be able to finish your first book in about five days to a week.

When it comes to choosing 80/20 actions for habits, your job is extremely simple. The activity that will have the most impact in you acquiring the habit is the habit itself. In this case, reading every day for the same approximate period of time is the action that will have the most impact on your outcome, and that's the only 80/20 action you need.

Examining Different Areas of Your Life

The three steps laid out earlier can be applied to almost all areas of your life. In the following sections, we'll identify five of the most important ones that probably need the 80/20 treatment. These are your relationships, habits, business/studies, health and the activities that take up the rest of your time. You could say that these are the 80-20 of your life situations and circumstances. Here is how you'll want to go about analyzing them.

Our first area is **relationships**. These don't just include romantic pairings, but friendships as well. Various studies from premier institutions like Oxford and Cornell Universities have found that the average person has hundreds of friends on social media networks. However, the number of people we consider close to us can still be counted on one hand, just as it could be in the 1980s, a simpler time.

If you were to go through your friends or follower lists, its highly likely that you too would realize that all those people whom you added to keep your friendship from receding into oblivion never cross your mind. Eighty percent of your happiness and enjoyment probably comes from a few close friends, a significant other or spouse, and maybe some intimate business connections.

Seeing large numbers of friends on social media may give us the illusion that we're staying connected to all of these hundreds of people, or that we can count on them when we really need it. However, reality is likely to be disappointing, and somewhere we all realize that. As the research of Oxford's Professor Dunbar shows, this only makes us unhappy because while social media tells us we have many, many friends, we really don't. Find out who the most important ones are and eliminate the rest.

To apply the steps we covered in a previous section: set some goals when it comes to your social life or relationships. For example, you may decide that you want to nurture and deepen a connection you have with two or three particular people (or drop some especially toxic friends!). Once you've established your goal, you can identify the 80/20 path to take, i.e. find the way to get the most rewards for the lowest effort. For example, signing up to a regular gym class with a friend means you get to interact with them routinely, without having to work to make plans with them again and again.

Finally, identify the 80/20 actions you need to take. In our example, you may notice that most of your feelings of connection with a particular friend come from long, one-on-one conversations, whereas other kinds of interaction don't bring you any closer. This means that when it comes down to it, you prioritize this kind of meeting with them and feel OK with dropping activities that you know don't serve your ultimate goal to get closer to them.

Next come our **habits**. Acquiring new habits and dumping old ones can be extraordinarily hard. We're all used to doing certain things in a certain way for various reasons that have nothing to do with actual usefulness. The 80/20 principle tells us that the majority of what we busy ourselves with during the day adds little or nothing to our success or well-being, which instead rests on just 20% of our daily routines.

When we ignore the principle, we might refrain from creating routines at all to avoid being boxed in and allow for more flexibility, or we may multitask even though countless studies have shown that this actually makes us less productive and can even lead to a drop in overall IQ. (Paul 2012) Yet we continue because we feel like we're getting more things done at once.

You need a clear, objective appraisal of what exactly you fill your time with, day in and day out. One advisable way to go about this is to journal everything you do for a few days and rate your activities on a scale of 1-10 based on the benefit and ease they provided. So, if you ate bacon for breakfast, ask yourself if that improved your life in any way. It probably didn't. What can you replace the bacon with? Maybe some eggs, fruits, or something else you like eating that is also healthy.

Similarly, if you woke up late in the morning, ask yourself whether that practice is making you more productive. It could well be despite all the advice on waking up early. You need to choose what works for you and build on those habits. This doesn't mean you need to eliminate every unproductive habit. The goal here is to make more room for the 20% of most important habits you follow or should be following, while eliminating most which can be replaced.

If you've identified a truly significant habit (i.e. the 20%) then you can budget all your energy, focus and willpower on making sure that those things get done, no matter what. But if you know that a particular habit is useful, but not exactly critical (i.e. the 80%), then you can be a bit more flexible.

For example, if daily exercise is one of the biggest contributors to your feeling of well-being, you can make sure that you exercise first thing in the morning, before you do anything else. If time is tight, you can compromise on other things—but never on daily exercise. You simultaneously work hard and with diligence (on what matters) but cut yourself slack when needed (on what matters less).

The third important area we'll consider is **business**. A large portion of the next chapter is going to be dedicated to the use of the Pareto rule in businesses and productivity, but for now, suffice it to say that business allows for the most methodical application of the 80/20 principle. There are a multiplicity of tools and software that allow you to track the

20% of customers buying most of your products, the 20% of employees generating the most sales, and the 20% of marketing that's converting the most leads. By collating all this data, you can easily find out what you should keep and build on, as well as what can be done away with.

Now we come to **hobbies and leisure**. Most of the conversation surrounding the Pareto principle focuses on productivity and efficiency. While that is undeniably important, we also need to know how we can have fun and engage in activities that make us happy in ways that maximize our satisfaction. This in turn makes us more likely to be creative and productive when we work, because we feel like we've spent enough quality time on ourselves.

Ask yourself, does 20% of my leisure time provide 80% of my happiness? If yes, which 20% is that? This part is quite simple. There's a small chance you might think *no, most of my leisure activities contribute equally to my happiness*. In fact, that's a tempting retort to the implementation of 80/20 in any aspect of your life. But it's usually just not the truth. We all certainly prefer certain activities and even people far more than others.

Lastly, we have our **health**. There's some overlap between your habits and health, but here we'll primarily focus on nutrition and physical exercise. If you're someone who enjoys working out, jogging, playing sports, etc., each of these contributes to your overall happiness along with your fitness. To assess your health, ask yourself two questions. First, do 20% of your workouts lead to 80% of your gains or weight loss? Second, take a negative approach to nutrition and ask, do 20% of the foods you eat contribute to 80% of your weight gain? Overall, what 20% of actions can you take that will result in 80% of weight being lost or fitness goals achieved?

The answers to these questions should tell you a lot about how to become healthier. You might play a lot of sports and yet fail to observe too much weight loss or muscle gain despite how exhausted it leaves you. Depending on your preferences, working out at the gym might be a better solution for both of them, and so you might want to include that more extensively in the 20% that gives you 80% of your results.

Similarly, you might notice that consuming things like sugary beverages, chips, processed foods, alcohol, fast food, chocolate, etc., is what's preventing you from achieving your health goals. This happens even when you're ingesting these items in moderation. You might get away with retaining one or two of these calorie-rich foods, but you'll need to cut out most of it.

There are a few other ways you can use the 80/20 principle regarding your health too. For example, ask yourself if 20% of the foods you consume drain 80% of your energy. Many of these 20% foods are likely to coincide with the ones causing your weight gain, and reducing your intake of them will leave you with the energy to get much more done every day.

Lastly, you can also ask yourself which 20% of your exercises while working out seem to be contributing to your muscle mass/weight loss. Once you've identified them, try finding a more difficult version online and do those. So if you've found squats helpful, start doing pistol squats or Bulgarian split squats. As a more general matter, remember that we are trying to shift our thinking toward the 20% of activities as a whole that move the needle— the lowest effort with the highest reward. For many of us, this might be as simple as replacing all beverages with water, walking sixty minutes a day, and skipping the midnight snack. Start with the foundations.

Goal Setting Using the 80/20 Principle

We've now covered the three major steps of applying the Pareto principle, and in this section as well as the next two we'll be going into further detail about each step individually to give you even more ways of using them into your pursuits.

Brian Tracy, another major proponent of the 80/20 rule, has an extremely useful framework for goal setting and starting off the process of using this principle in your life. The first step in this process is to take a piece of paper and write down ten of your most coveted goals. Once you have them, ask yourself: if you could only achieve one of these, which one would have the greatest net positive impact on your life?

Once you've identified the goal, set it aside, and ask yourself the same question with the goals you have remaining. These are your 20% most important goals, and you can follow the same process even if you have more or less goals in mind.

While selecting your goals, it's important not to be intimidated by tough aspirations. These are usually tough precisely because they add the most value. It might be tempting to clear up the small goals first. These may make you feel like you can then singularly focus on the big achievement, but this often doesn't transpire, and we end up putting off the major goals for the future. This can easily become a habit wherein you become accustomed to handling low-value tasks first, which many times doesn't leave enough time for the major ones. As such, it's better to bite the bullet and, in the words of

Tracy, "eat the biggest frog first." If needed, devote all your energies exclusively to that one goal instead of five small ones.

There are several ways you can make the pursuit of tough goals easier. For one, try and find ways to make achieving them fun. So, if you're looking to eat healthy despite being a foodie, try and find delicious recipes that include beneficial ingredients. These do exist, and if you take the effort to find them, you can kill two birds with one stone.

Another method is to tell others about your goals. This sets up a self-reinforcing mechanism of accountability, because we're often more afraid of disappointing others than ourselves. So, if you want to bulk up, you might want to tell a close friend about it. They're bound to notice if you look the same two or three months later, and that will act as motivation for you to follow through on your goals.

A third technique is to divide your goals and actions into smaller, more manageable steps and track your progress religiously.

One last helpful tip for achieving your goals is to regularly question why you're bothering with them in the first place, and whether they align with your values. Values change over time, and your goals might feel less satisfying than they once did in accordance with your progress. Realign your goals according to your values and needs from time to time. This will reinforce a sense of purpose and importance regarding what you're trying to achieve.

Low Effort, High Reward: the 80/20 Path

We've discussed the four different paths to every goal in an earlier section, and now we'll address an invaluable tool to help you chart the 80/20 path. This is the Action Priority Matrix (APM) (Elsey 2019). The APM is a simple diagramming technique to help you choose and prioritize activities based on their importance. It involves a simple graph, wherein the y axis denotes impact, and the x axis highlights efforts needed for the activities. To obtain a grid, draw two lines from the middle of both axes.

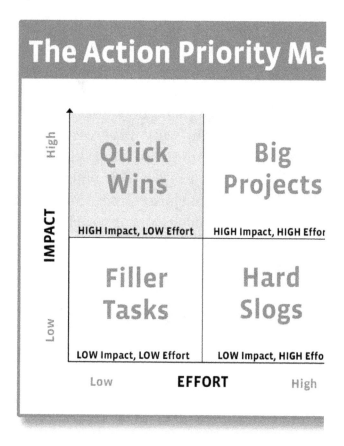

**The Action Priority Ma**

|  | | |
|---|---|---|
| **IMPACT** High | **Quick Wins** <br> HIGH Impact, LOW Effort | **Big Projects** <br> HIGH Impact, HIGH Effo |
| Low | **Filler Tasks** <br> LOW Impact, LOW Effort | **Hard Slogs** <br> LOW Impact, HIGH Effo |

Low    **EFFORT**    High

This will give you four types of activities. On the bottom left, you'll have the "Fill In's." To its right, we have something called "Thankless Tasks." Directly above it comes "Major Projects," and to the left of that we end with "Quick Wins." These are similar to the four paths we mentioned earlier. Quick Wins are analogous to high impact, low effort tasks, while Major Projects are high impact, high effort. Thankless Tasks are low impact, high effort activities, and Fill In's are low impact, low effort ones.

The similarities aside, this graphical representation serves a larger purpose. Not only will it help you identify which tasks and goals fall into which category, but also how to go about achieving them. It also makes for a great visual learning tool for picturing and planning your ideal course of action.

Start by making a list of all of your goals and activities involving them. Next, score all of these actions based on how much impact they'll create when completed, as well as how much effort they need. You can use an A-F, a 1-10 scale, or others depending on your preferences. Now, plot all the activities on the graph based on your scores. You're likely to fill at least three of the four grid boxes, if not all of them.

Use your denotations to prioritize your activities. Quick Wins should be at the top of your list—these are the activities that must receive the bulk of your efforts. The rest of your time should primarily be spent on Major Projects. If you can't delegate the Fill In's, do them next, but these shouldn't concern you too much if you've completed your Quick Wins and Major Projects. Lastly, eliminate all Thankless Tasks as far as you possibly can.

As you start following this scheme of prioritization, there are some things you should keep in mind. While completing Quick Wins, reserve ample amounts of time for doing Major Projects. It's easy to get sucked in and slack off while doing Quick Wins because of how rewarding they can be, but you'll want to avoid complacency.

Once you've reached your Major Projects, don't spend excessive amounts of time on them. Break them down into smaller parts and move on to other Major Projects if one seems too daunting and return to it later. Set time limits for doing Fill In's, and if you find yourself forced to do Thankless Tasks, break them down and delegate everything that you can.

Takeaways

- There are three useful steps to follow in implementing the 80/20 rule for maximum effect. First, identify your goals by writing down a list, but selecting only the two or three most important ones—these are the ones that inspire passion and productivity, and align with your values and life purpose. These are the goals that have the highest chance of creating happiness, although it's wise to regularly check in with your values, as they can change with time.
- The next step is to identify the 80/20 you'll take. Look at your chosen goals and categorize them as either low effort, low reward (filler tasks), high effort, high reward (big projects), high effort, low reward (hard slogs), or low effort, high reward (quick wins, or the 80/20 path that you want to take first). Once you've decided which path is easiest and

most rewarding, you can prioritize your actions accordingly.

- The third step is to identify these tasks and actions. You can get an idea of useful tasks by looking to other successful people, but beware: you may find success doing the exact opposite! Once you've identified useful actions, make as many of them habitual/automatic as possible by building them into routines.

- These three steps can apply to any area of life, such as relationships, habits, business or study, health and miscellaneous activities. By choosing the most important goal, and identifying the most effective and elegant way to achieve that objective, you are essentially outlining the swiftest path to the outcome that will give you the most satisfaction and reward, no matter what area of life you apply the method to.

In relationships, for example, you can focus your attentions on that small handful of people who genuinely bring the most happiness to your life, and similarly, you can look at your daily habits and ask honestly what daily actions are really bringing you closer to happiness and success, and which aren't. Where hobbies are concerned, you can frequently examine your activities and ask where the best 20% of your experience actually comes from, and with your health you can identify and eliminate your single worst habit, or build on your most effective one.

# Chapter 4. The 80/20 of Professional Success

Many of the most successful companies in history such as IBM, Ford, Apple, Microsoft, and others have all exploited the Pareto principle to great success. What makes this rule such a good fit for businesses?

One answer is that the assumptions of the 80/20 rule—like the idea that a small number of factors causes the greatest impact on outcomes—closely mirrors behaviors observed in the marketplace. For example, some businesses are inevitably much better than others at satisfying customer needs and demands. Due to their efficiency, these businesses swiftly capture an increasing share of the market, which allows them to command higher prices for their products or services.

This superior ability to satisfy needs stems from their capacity to minimize costs, as well as maximize profits through a variety of strategies. Both of these involve the 80/20 principle; in fact, many of the best business practices invariably employ the 80/20 principle even without knowing it.

As these companies become successful, their higher profits allow for more reinvestment into products, better marketing efforts, more innovation, improved compensation for employees, etc. The principle, when applied consistently, can lead to exponential effects that really drive success. The 80/20 rule essentially gives shape to the iterative act of observing, adjusting and observing again to continuously fine tune toward only those tactics that really work. This eventually leads some companies to a position wherein they become a part of the 20% suppliers that provide 80% of products.

Though this is just a crude sketch of how a company comes to occupy a large market share, you can see the myriad ways in which the 80/20 rule figures into the process. At every single level of business, be it the employees you hire, the products you sell, the way you handle operations, marketing, customers, etc., all of it is influenced by the Pareto principle.

The difference between a successful and failing business is that the former is better at using this rule to rectify imbalances between efforts or inputs and returns. This chapter will focus on the ways in which you can reduce inputs while increasing returns in key parts of your business. This will have a reverberating effect that eventually spreads, creating a positive impact overall on the productivity and profits of your venture.

An 80/20 Businesses

We've highlighted the widespread prevalence of the 80/20 rule in the world of business. Now, we're going to elaborate on the specific ways and areas where this rule can be applied to help your business grow at an exponential rate.

The first major area where this principle can aid your business is **decision-making**. Since the 1950s, the role of expert analysis in businesses has seen a meteoric rise as companies increasingly rely on short-term trends, be it in the stock market or otherwise, to gain an advantage over their competition. Yet the sheer amount of corporate staff dedicated to this function are starting to be dismantled because businesses have realized that most decisions are not likely to have much of an impact.

In fact, most important decisions for a business aren't actively made at all. These involve situations with disgruntled top employees, underestimating competition, not capitalizing on your own innovations enough, etc. No amount of data-gathering and analysis can help with issues like these, but they are phenomena that can greatly affect the functioning of your business.

Instead, the best thing to do here is to gather 80% of the required data and conduct 80% of the analysis in the first 20% of the time available. The time limit has been instituted because decisions usually need to be taken quickly, and given the unimportance of most of them, it isn't worth spending too much time on them. If the decision you make works, double down on it. If it doesn't, don't be afraid of experimenting and trying again. In addition, spend 80% of your time analyzing the most important 20% of decisions.

Look at the risks involved and any (genuine) time limits. If a problem is time-critical as well as highly risky (i.e. there is a high cost to making the wrong decision), then it forms part of the 20% and most of your efforts should go to solving it. On the other hand, if a wrong decision has very little effect or can easily be reversed, you save time and energy by simply making a decision, any decision, and adjusting afterwards as necessary. In fact, acting quickly may be better since it gives you more data to work with in future.

As such, the main takeaway here is not to spend too much time making the decision itself, but to take future decisions based on how previous actions went. This doesn't mean you can randomly choose any option and wait for the results; data does have a role to play here. However, the important thing is to not spend too much time collecting the data and analyzing it. We seldom have all the facts, and often we only learn key information once the process is already underway. Let go of perfectionism. Take 80% of what you have, decide on which course seems most prudent, and make a choice confidently.

A second area is **project management**. In recent times, project management has become an extraordinarily complex process. Often, a single project acts as an umbrella for several subsidiary projects all working simultaneously. This has a major impact on the overall efficiency of the enterprise, because projects obey the law of organizational complexity. The more a project tries to accomplish, the more effort you need to put in. However, the increase is nowhere near proportional—the effort required increases manifold.

This points to the first way in which the Pareto principle figures into project management. If 80% of a project's success comes from 20% of the effort put into it, the problem we've highlighted makes the other 80% of effort enormously convoluted. The simple solution is to do away with the remaining effort altogether by restricting the end goal to one high-value task, which in turn reduces the input needed and ensures more gets done with less work.

Another way to implement the rule here is to assign your team small time periods to accomplish their goal. This forces them to tap into the 20% time spent that results in 80% of the result. Desperate times call for creative solutions, and pushing your team in healthy ways will inspire exceptional results. This is not as stressful as it sounds—by deliberately adding some constraints, your employees can be inspired into action sooner, and a time limit naturally encourages a sharper focus on what will really bring results.

The next relevant area of business for applying the 80/20 principle is **sales**. This is arguably one of the most important components of your business because it determines your overall profits. To boost sales, the main thing you need to focus on is the people making those sales. These are your top performers, the 20% that are bringing in 80% of your revenue. But while it's easy to identify who these 20% are through basic data advantage, there's more to do here than just letting the unproductive ones go.

If your business is successful as is, you might be tempted to go with the old adage "if it ain't broke, don't fix it." While this is good advice in other areas, it's a surefire way to stagnation for businesses. Instead, this is what you'll want to do once you've identified your top salesmen and let go of the rest.

Firstly, keep your employees happy, and build personal relationships with them instead of simply raising their pay. Next, you'll want to identify what exactly it is that makes them the top 20% of salesmen in your company. It's likely that 80% of their success came from what they spent 20% of their worktime doing. Find out what they did in that 20% time and get your other employees to adopt the same methods. Lastly, look after the 20% customers purchasing 80% of your products by teaching your salesforce to rank them and spend more time on them.

The next component of your business where the Pareto principle proves invaluable is **cutting costs**. All organizations have enormous potential for cost cutting and creating more value for their customers. They can actualize this potential in two ways: eliminating low-value activities that eat up resources and simplifying their business model.

Remember that 80% of what is important is supported by just 20% of the overall expenditure into your business. Find out where the remaining 80% of your money is going and identify the areas that have the biggest cost-reduction potential. Get a better idea of which of your company's pursuits are providing the bulk of value for you and your customer and cut the rest.

Let's consider an example. Say you run a publishing firm and your manager tells you that your typesetting costs are 30% over your budget. You receive several reasons for this, such as delays by the author, delays by proofreaders, the book manuscript is longer than planned, etc. What you'll want to do now is to set a time period, ideally a few months, and observe all sources of excessive typesetting overruns, their frequency and the costs involved. You'll likely observe that 80% of the extra cost comes from 20% of typesetting overruns. Do what you can to minimize these, and you've successfully used the 80/20 rule to cut costs. The few typesetting errors that were causing most of your added expenditure have been eliminated.

These are only a few areas of your business that can be improved by using the 80/20 principle, but they're among the most relevant. As you can see, the general framework across areas remains the same.

Identify the 20% providing the most value and get rid of the remaining 80%.

To assess your business using the Pareto principle, we'll start by looking at the four different categories of business that are most relevant to revenue generation. These are: a) products and product groups, b) customers, c) splits that are specifically relevant for your business, like distribution channels, and d) your competitive segment.

Let's start with **products**. Your success in assessing various parts of your business is heavily reliant on you having the data to reach informed conclusions. For this category, first you'll need to segregate all your products into groups. You can choose to analyze them over the past month, quarter, or year depending on which segment you believe will give you the most accurate picture of their profitability. Next, create columns listing the product groups, how many sales you've accrued on each, the profit you made from selling them, and the return on sales by percentage. Make sure you calculate the total income and sales overall as well.

Once you have all the data, now you need to look at the numbers and figure out which 20% of sales accounts for 80% of your profit. Keep in mind that 80 and 20 may not be the best numbers for your business, and you can use other lopsided distributions as well. Say you have six product groups, and the first two make up 65% of your profits, yet only 17% of your sales. What you can do is redirect the efforts of your salesforce by asking them to concentrate on increasing the sales of those two product groups without worrying about the rest. If they succeed, you'll see a monumental rise in profits.

Furthermore, you could raise prices of the other product groups or cut costs by reducing your orders of the other groups. You might even want to consider eliminating the least profitable product groups.

Coming to your **customers**, analyzing them will require you to make a table very similar to the one you made for your products. You'll want to segregate your customers based on how much they buy from you and how much it costs you to serve them. The latter can be based on whether they drive a hard bargain and force you to reduce prices, customer service costs, etc.

These are some customer types you might encounter. Type 1 purchases a lot and gives you very high margins, but also costs a lot to serve. Type 2 also purchases a lot, but costs much less to serve. Type 3 bargains a lot on price and is also expensive to serve. Once you've identified which types frequent your business, account for them in your table and list how much of sales they account for, the income they generate for you, and the return on sales from these conversions.

Analyzing these datapoints should reveal not one but two uneven distributions. First, you're likely to see that the most profitable customer type generates a small percentage of the revenue but a sizeable portion of the profits. Second, the most profitable 20-30% of customers overall most probably generates 80-90% of your profits. The results of your analysis should encourage you to try and gain more customers of the type that are most profitable. So, if your most profitable customers are distributors, you should concentrate your outreach and marketing efforts on distributors more than, say, less profitable customers such as export accounts.

Other **relevant splits,** which is our third category, will vary widely depending on your business. If you run a consultancy firm, this split could be between large and small projects. You could also choose a split between old, intermediate, and new clients.

This is one that any company could calculate for their business, especially since old clients are generally the moneymakers because they purchase steady amounts of product and are cheap to serve. New clients who don't turn into long-term clients tend to become loss-makers, and if this is the case for you, marketing efforts can be concentrated based on how likely your target is to become a long-term client.

The last category, your **competitive segments**, is arguably the most important. Competitive segments are parts of your business where you encounter different competitors or different competitive dynamics. To identify the competitive segments of your business, take any of the other three categories—products, customer, or another relevant split—and ask yourself two questions.

First, do you face a different customer in this part of your business compared to others? If yes, then that part of your business is a competitive segment in itself. So, if you sell cosmetics but also watches, your business has two different competitive segments because those products ensure you're up against two different types of competitors.

Your second should be: Do you and your competitor have the same ratio of sales and market share in the various segments your business belongs to? You might also face the same competitor in different segments, and if so, comparing market share for different products becomes immensely important.

On the flip side, it's possible that all your business specializes in a particular type of product and thus faces only one competitor.

Once you have your different segments, the process follows a similar trajectory as the other categories. Draw up a table with the segments, sales for each of them, the profits made on cumulative sales, and the return on sales in percentage. Once you've accumulated all this data, you're likely to observe that a few of your segments bring in 80-90% of your profits despite accounting for only a small percentage of sales.

Based on your results, you can then reorganize the efforts of your business to maximize sales of the segments that are most profitable for you. However, unlike the other categories, don't be quick to discard or eliminate the comparatively unprofitable segments. If the segment is an attractive one with a high potential for profits in the future, you might well want to dedicate more effort there as well.

The 80/20 of Higher Profits

By now, you've learned the various ways in which the Pareto principle can help your business, as well as how to use it to assess your business and observe the areas that could use reorganization. It's time to go one step further and discuss some ways in which you can use the principle to maximize your profits. In this section, we'll focus on three key areas that we haven't yet given much attention: marketing, manpower, and leadership.

Our first tip has to do with **content marketing**. Content marketing is the creation and distribution of content to attract and retain specific demographics within your audience. If you don't already engage in this form of marketing, it can be a powerful tool for growing your business because of its emphasis on relevant content that is specifically geared toward the people it is aimed at.

Alternatively, if you've been using it for a while, you might've observed that 80% of your leads and traffic come from 20% of your content assets. Find out which of your assets are performing the best and create more content of the same kind. You can also expand them by turning those assets into long-form guides, essentially repurposing the same content in multiple formats.

The next strategy is related to **SEO and keywords**. Businesses tend to spend inordinate amounts of time in coming up with a keyword strategy. However, it's likely that a few of your keywords are driving most of your incoming traffic. The ratio here is often even more lopsided than 80% of traffic coming in from 20% of your keywords. In fact, it's possible that just one or two of your top keywords are generating anywhere between a third to half of all your traffic. Like with content marketing, discover these keywords using tools like Google Analytics and come up with more content based around them.

When it comes to your marketing strategy overall and the various channels you utilize, be it ad words, content marketing, banners, retargeting, etc., a few of these channels are probably generating most of your traffic and thus conversions. Focus on the channels providing you with the most value for your investment.

Coming to **manpower**, we've already discussed several things you can do to get the most out of your top performers, and here we'll suggest a few more tips to this end.

The first thing you'll want to do is identify what **motivates** your superstars to perform their best for your organization. This could be your compensation structure, your flexible working hours, student debt assistance, or something else. Identify these motivators on an individual basis and, if possible, give them more of it. This tip is consistent with the general strategy of awarding special perks to your top performers to maximize their good performance.

Besides disproportionately awarding these top employees, you also need to spend a lot more time **listening** to them than simply telling them what to do. When you give top employees a chance to lead the path, they push themselves to perform even better. While you might spend more time instructing your low performers, spend 80% of your time listening to the best-performing ones.

You can take this tip one step further by allowing them to set their own objectives and identify key steps toward achieving them. Companies like Google and Intel follow this strategy called OKRs (Objectives and Key Results) to increase productivity among top performers. This will allow you to save a lot of time that would've otherwise been spent listening to or instructing them. Through this strategy, you simply have to approve of their plans after understanding their thinking process behind it.

These strategies on managing your top performers are closely related to the next most important application of the 80/20 rule, which is **leadership**. Here, it's important to know what kind of qualities an 80/20 leader possesses. First, such a leader is introspective and knows the right questions to ask his employees and him or herself. Unsurprisingly, most of these questions involve the Pareto principle, be it regarding customers, resources, management, etc.

Second, an 80/20 leader emphasizes simplicity. This figures into everything they do, be it work instructions, project management, reports, etc. Third, an 80/20 manager is decisive in that they have a certain vision and roadmap for their business, and they arrange everything to ensure the realization of that vision. Lastly, such a leader is focused on the 20% that matters and spends almost all of his or her time on making the most of it.

As you can see, the Pareto principle figures heavily in creating a certain type of leader who is adept at concentrating and arranging resources in maximally productive ways. This is all because the 80/20 rule is such an effective way to assess every aspect of your business. There is always a way you can use the principle to improve some aspect or area of your organization; you just need to find it by asking the right questions of yourself and the relevant people involved in your venture. This strategy has worked for many of the most successful companies on earth, and it's sure to work for you as well.

## 80/20 Careers

So far in this chapter we've looked at ways to improve the profitability of your business with the assumption that you're the one calling the shots. You're responsible for all the decisions, and you have the authority to influence the workings of a company adequately enough to effect change.

However, now we'll look at businesses from the other side of the fence—the employees' end of things. Even if responsibilities like management, decision-making, analysis, etc., aren't part of your job description, there are still several ways in which the 80/20 rule can help you be a better and more successful employee. In this section, we'll talk about how you can use the principle to effectively manage your time, and increase your productivity as well.

Richard Koch has drawn a very insightful dichotomy between time management and a **time revolution**. Applying the 80/20 principle to your time does not mean that you simply need to use your time better, take less breaks, or spend more time planning the rest of it. All of that falls under time management.

Instead, the application of this rule entails a complete time revolution, which is a fundamental shift in the way you think about time itself. Time management comes with the constant pressure of using your time effectively. But this doesn't improve the way you use your time, it only brings frustration, longer working hours, and an addiction to finding better and better ways to manage time.

The Pareto principle does away with these marginal improvements in the usage of our time. It refuses to accept that we can come up with a routine wherein 100% of our time can be used productively. Far from frantically doing the most in the least amount of time, this rule assumes that we have more than enough time to achieve all our important goals. This is because the principle operates with the assumption that time is cyclical, and not linear. It doesn't just come and go, forever lost to history; it comes repeatedly, bringing with it new opportunities to learn and improve.

To begin your time revolution, you'll need to change the way you approach your time, and there are a few things you can do to achieve this. Perhaps the most important step here is to dissociate the mental connection between effort and reward. It is also important to let go of the guilt that comes with time spent unproductively. The 20% of people who own 80% of wealth are also 20% of the workers/businessmen who enjoy their work 80% of the time.

A third way you can change your approach toward time is by taking ownership of it. If 20% of your time gives you 80% of your results, the remaining 80% of your time is likely being spent on tasks that were undertaken for others. Obviously, it isn't possible to rid yourself of obligations and completely avoid doing things for others, especially as an employee. However, the takeaway here is that you should spend your time in ways that you and you alone deem appropriate. Rather than merely finding creative ways to squeeze in as many non-essential activities as possible, ask yourself how you can shape your work so that you have more power to eliminate or delegate those non-essential tasks entirely.

Once you've given yourself some time to think these steps over and incorporate them into your mindset about time, you'll be ready for the next phase of your time revolution. This phase has everything to do with the 20% of your time that gives you 80% of your results. Start by identifying which 20% of your time is being spent most productively. Give yourself a few days to a week for observing this, and make sure to note down the times when you're most and least productive.

There are many tasks that are generally of high value and which are likelier than others to produce many times the output of the time you spend doing them. While assessing the ways you spend your time, you might well find a large degree of overlap between these general high-value tasks and the ones where you're at your most efficient.

These include tasks that further your assumed purpose in life, things you've always wanted to do, things that you already know will give you more results than the effort you put into them, and tasks where you're given free rein to apply your creativity. On the other hand, tasks that are a huge time-sink are those which you aren't very good at or don't enjoy doing. They could also be ones where your collaborators are inefficient, or tasks that can only be done a certain way and have no space for creativity.

This is not to say that you should never bother with tasks that you aren't already an expert in, or that you shouldn't spend some effort trying to improve a situation before abandoning it because it's not 100% as you'd like it. Rather, it's about realizing that you're in charge. Sometimes the best way to optimize something is to not do it at all!

As the common 80/20 wisdom goes, you'll need to double the time you spend on your high-value tasks while reducing time spent on the low-value ones. While this won't give you 160% of output, it will still increase your overall productivity exponentially. Try and delegate most of your low-value work, and work during times of the day you're most productive at. So if you're someone who likes sleeping in, waking up early to increase your productivity will likely not work.

One thing to keep in mind here is that, even with an awareness of the Pareto principle, it can be difficult to escape the tyranny of the 80/20 distribution wherein 80% of your time is spent on low-value tasks. The best way to ensure a good chance of breaking through this barrier is to spend your time in the most unconventional and eccentric manner as you can. Don't waste your time doing the decent things that are expected of you and weigh you down. Instead, think of all the ways you could do things differently than you do now, without making such a shift disorienting and impossibly difficult.

Here is an example of how this works. Let's say you're a consultant who has managed to earn millions of dollars from your job and you've now started your own venture. You'd be forgiven for thinking that your every waking moment will now in some way be spent on tasks related to this enterprise. Yet, you could quite as easily let your other employees work seventy to eighty hours a week and take a more laidback approach.

Obviously, this would make you a terrible boss and human being, but it does drive home the point that a lot of our assumptions about work, business and success are just that—assumptions. Truly thinking out of the box means questioning the old scripts, for example that a successful person is necessarily one who works themselves to death, or that if you achieve one level of efficiency and success you are compelled to immediately seek out the next level, forever.

The key to this approach is not to constantly be doing something all the time, but learning to delegate work between your top employees, who will likely themselves delegate it further. Remember, the 80/20 principle is one that requires a non-linear mindset—you are not necessarily being lazy by turning certain tasks down and refusing to constantly plow forward, any more than you are being effective by taking them on.

Attend only the most important meetings, set objectives that need to be met, provide ways for those objectives to be achieved, and let the others do the work. You may discover plenty of people who are still laboring under the misconception that endless "busywork" will lead to success. Try not to get sucked into the pointless bureaucracy that comes with this approach.

The most important thing you need to do is decide which tasks to delegate in the first place. If you've been reading this book attentively so far, you'll have an easy time selecting the most important ones using assessments of your business through the 80/20 principle. But how you spend the rest of your time is up to you. You could play golf, read novels, travel the world and do what your heart desires. The main barrier to overcome here is not the sheer amount of work itself, but the need to be constantly doing work to feel accomplished.

This last tip is in line with the previous one, and it is to remember to not be afraid of taking time off. If you feel burned out, overwhelmed, or excessively stressed, realize that 80% of your time is spent on expendable tasks anyway. Skipping some of them will do you absolutely no harm.

While the approach-related changes are something everyone can benefit from, some of these tips assume that you're capable and willing to undertake a time revolution. However, for a wide variety of reasons, that may not be feasible for you. If this sounds like you, you can still try to incorporate as many of the above tips as you can. 20% of your time spent will still produce 80% of your outcome. Below are few more techniques that will be useful to you.

The first most important thing you can do if a time revolution is unfeasible is to cut out all your distractions. This could be calls you receive, notifications on your phone, etc. The trickiest part of such distractions is that they appear to take only minutes of your time. However, several cognitive processes are involved in shutting down the task you're currently doing, switching to attending to these distractions, stopping them and restarting your original task.

You may only be on your phone for a minute, but your concentration and focus on your previous task take a hit in ways that take much longer to recover. In other words, it destroys your flow. To avoid consequent wastages of time, learn to eliminate such distractions altogether.

The second small but significant technique is to never lose track of your larger goal. Too often, we're disinterestedly completing some tasks with minimal focus just to get them over with. But this approach only ensures you take longer to do them and also degrades the quality of your work. By reminding yourself of *why* you're doing what you're doing, you can revive a sense of purpose in yourself and make better use of that time. However, if you can't find a good answer to that why, it may be time to make some changes to the tasks you spend substantial amounts of time on.

The way you use your time is intimately connected with the second biggest way to make a difference in your career using the Pareto principle, and that is by improving your **productivity**. While all the advice on time will indirectly improve your productivity as well, there is one major thing you can do to take your efficiency to the next level.

First, you must know that the first 20% of time spent on a project yields 80% of its results. The more time you spend on it beyond the first 20%, the lower your output becomes. This makes it imperative that you maximize your gains early, and there are multiple ways to do this.

To consider an example, say you have to create a webpage within ten days. You spend the first two of these coding and creating a working website that is then ready to test. It would be natural to think that you've completed the bulk of your task and that completion is about to follow suit. However, you'll likely realize that it will take another week just to iron out all the bugs, polishing your design and interface, testing it on different browsers, etc. In the first 20% of your time, you almost completed the entire project. But the other 80% was spent on low-value tasks that would normally take far less time.

Most things you do have a similar set of low-value tasks that individually seem small, but take up large chunks of your time when combined together. Use the 80/20 principle to minimize this unnecessary loss.

The best way to reduce these time wastages is by getting feedback. This can be from anyone, from a client, to your spouse, friends, coworkers, anyone willing to give you their time. This way, you'll quickly rectify errors without spending too much time on them, or completing other parts of your projects that are linked to these errors and would otherwise have to be redone. Use the 30% feedback rule and ask for advice once you're 30% done with the task you've undertaken.

Another related tip that will make you more productive is knowing when to move on from a particular task. This is especially relevant for those who have jobs in more artistic fields because the temptation to improve your work through minor tweaks can be difficult to move past. However, the more time you spend toward the end stages of a project, the less likely you are to cause any monumental change in your work. Perfectionists will likely disagree, but you can save yourself a lot of time by knowing when there isn't anything more to add and moving on to your next task.

Takeaways

- In business, the 80/20 model works because it closely mirrors the way the market itself behaves. Using the 80/20 principle can lead to compounding efficiencies that quickly cause the business to represent the 20% most successful businesses.
- The principle applies to decision making, and cuts short "analysis

paralysis" or time wasted on deliberation over the unimportant 80%. Instead, it's wise to act sooner and get feedback quickly, so as to course correct as soon as possible. In project management, the principle can help to slice away at useless organizational complexity, for example by identifying only those actions that lead to a single high-value goal. With employees, the principle helps you identify the top performers so they can be supported, and by the same token pinpoint inefficiencies and waste, so that costs can be cut, and the biggest inefficiency culprits found and eliminated.

- The principle can help you appraise the functioning of your business in areas such as products (categorize each according to their profitability), customers (identify those who purchase a lot but cost a little to maintain, and downplay the reverse), splits (such as the proportion of old vs. new clients, big vs. small jobs, etc.), and competition (asking who they are and how they compare to you can help you adjust your strategy accordingly).

- For employees, the 80/20 rules can help shape time-management efforts, but goes a step further and inspires "time revolution"—rethinking time entirely, and undoing the assumption that effort is always proportional to outcome. This means delegation without guilt, using time wisely and not just being productive, and frequently identifying high and low-value tasks for yourself. It also means seeking feedback often and early so you can adjust sooner rather than later, after you've already wasted time on unimportant tasks.

The way you choose to use the Pareto Principle in your own business or as an employee will depend greatly on the business, your role in it and your ultimate goals. Nevertheless, the 80/20 principle can improve almost every business or work decision, from your content marketing or SEO strategy to the way in which you identify and reward top performers, to your leadership approach in general.

# Chapter 5. 80/20 For a Better You

It's often the case that when we get off from our jobs to finally come home and spend time relaxing or on leisure activities we enjoy, our minds are still racing. We're occupied with thoughts and worries that are unrelated to our professional lives. This could include your finances, taking care of your relationships, the long list of tasks that you've been putting off, etc. In the previous sections, we've covered how you can minimize stress at work by getting more work done in less time using the 80/20 principle and being the uber-productive self that you've probably always wanted to be.

Now, we're going to discuss how you can do the same thing at home. There are several things we do as part of our routine lives which take time away from activities we enjoy doing. Depending on your lifestyle, you may not be left with a single minute where you can breathe easy and put everything else aside. This has a significant impact on our happiness levels because it leaves us frustrated and feeling powerless, as we don't feel like we control our own lives.

With the 80/20 principle, you can take back control of your life and set yourself free. While we'll cover several areas in your life that can use the 80/20 treatment, there's a certain way of thinking underlying the application of this principle. Without adopting this specific approach, you'll only be able to apply the rule in generic ways that won't be conducive to getting the most out of it. Conversely, 80/20 thinking will go a long way in helping you tailor the principle and its applications to the idiosyncrasies of your lifestyle.

So, what is 80/20 thinking outside of the business world? Though this principle had its origins in economics and has most often been used in workplaces and for business, it is applicable for other areas too—although in a slightly adapted form. When used in our personal lives, the 80/20 principle is more like an attitude or approach; a particular orientation that guides our decision making, goals, values and behavior. This attitude has four major features in that it is *reflective, unconventional, hedonistic,* and *non-linear*. We'll go over each feature below.

Firstly, 80/20 thinking is **reflective** in that it overwhelmingly focuses on *you* and what suits *your* needs while still being efficient and productive. We're often taking the preferences and conveniences of others into account much more than we should, and 80/20 thinking strongly discourages this. If you remember the three steps framework for applying the 80/20 rule that we discussed earlier, reflection and introspection is often what will help you come up with your 80/20 actions.

This way of thinking is **unconventional** in that it refuses to take conventional wisdom for granted if it doesn't work for you. It encourages us to do away with all the things we do because they're known to generally work for a majority of the population.

How many self-help books have you seen that hold up various successful people as examples for how you should behave—with no consideration for whether their methods suit you as an individual or not? This could be things like waking up early, journaling every day, following a rigid routine, etc. Thinking unconventionally is not about being a rebel just for the sake of it, but about finding out what happiness and success look like for *you*.

Next, this approach is **hedonistic** because of its emphasis on pleasure and enjoying yourself. Too often the 80/20 rule is associated with just being more productive and efficient, and that is definitely one its biggest advantages. But the intention is not to run our personal lives like ultra-efficient sweatshops. We can use these ideas to make money or save time, but in a more abstract sense, we can optimize anything, including feelings of happiness, purpose, satisfaction, meaning and creative expression.

In this sense, we are still talking about productivity and efficiency, but the reason behind being more productive is not just for its own sake, but to give you space to enjoy yourself. To live a more fulfilling and elegant life. "Hedonism" here refers to the overall point of doing any of this—because, on some level, it feels good and makes us happy.

Lastly, 80/20 thinking is **non-linear** because it refuses to be boxed in by the conventions that define linear thinking. When anything bad happens in our lives, we tend to try and find the undesirable cause behind it. If our business isn't doing well, it's because the market is doing poorly. If we can't find a job it's because companies just aren't hiring.

But thinking this way often leaves us frustrated because the underlying cause is usually beyond our control. Try as we might to work around the margins, it rarely has any substantial impact on our problems.

With 80/20 thinking, we refuse to focus on all that's bad, instead concentrating on the few good things that can be exploited to our benefit.

When applied to private aspects of our life like relationships or personal issues, the principle can help us hone in on our core needs, develop gratitude for the "resources" we have, refine our values and commit to actually creating a life that supports those values. This kind of purposeful living is just not as possible when you're unfocused or haphazard.

All of these characteristics point toward three essential components of 80/20 thinking: the Pareto principle itself, finding 80/20 paths and actions that are tailored to you, and acting with your happiness and not simply expediency in mind. As we explore the different areas of your personal life that are ripe for applying the 80/20 rule, keep these features in mind to personalize your path forward.

80/20 Personal Finance

Personal finance is easily one of the biggest worries in any adult's life. Be it keeping your expenditures under control, tracking and managing your investments, maintaining a budget, ensuring you save enough, or something else, a lot of money is at stake. This makes any decision related to finance an anxiety-driven one. However, if you can learn to utilize the 80/20 rule while making key decisions, a lot of this anxiety can be alleviated. You'll be surer of your outcomes, more confident in your management of your finances, and most likely much richer as a result.

There are three main areas of personal finance where the 80/20 rule can provide you with rich dividends, quite literally. These are your investments, expenditures, and savings. We'll explore these in the same order.

It's no secret that **investments**, and not high employment income, is the key to becoming wealthy. The earlier you start investing, the longer your few good investments can provide you with good returns. As with the other areas of your life, 20% of your investments are going to generate 80% of your profits. What we need to do is find the most productive 20% investments you can possibly make, and determine how to go about doing this.

The very first thing you'll want to do when it comes to investments is to take charge of them and make them yourself. When you take the help of advisers and money managers, you minimize the chances of reaping the superior rewards that come with discovering and investing in the few high-performing assets that generate most of your profits. Instead, such managers tend to take a much safer approach while absorbing a lot of your profits in the process. They minimize risk by investing in a broad spectrum of media such as stocks, bonds, real estate, etc. However, the first tenet of enjoying superior returns through the Pareto principle is building an unbalanced portfolio.

Unbalanced portfolios lead to the second step of our process, which is to restrict your investments to only one medium: the stock market. This is primarily because investing in the stock market requires the least expertise. Most of the other options will require you to spend substantial amounts of time studying them and then making informed decisions. However, you can invest exclusively in blue-chip stocks that are safe, well-established, and have a reliable history of performance and still reap extreme rewards.

The key to getting the most out of these blue-chip stocks is to invest in them for the long-term. There's no need to move your stocks in and out of your portfolio unnecessarily unless they're guaranteed to lose you money. Invest in stocks with at least the next decade or two in mind. Investing for the short-term takes you into territory where you're making unreliable gambles. This could well lead to the opposite outcome than you're looking for, and so it makes sense for you to refrain from risks you don't need to take.

Another tip for investing that heavily relies on the Pareto principle is value investing.

Value investing is the practice wherein you purchase stocks when the market as a whole or particular stocks are valued much lower than they're worth. So, if the market is low and most people are hesitant to invest, that's when you should be investing the big bucks into the market. Conversely, when everyone is keen on investing, that's when you should be wary and hold back your funds. Strategies like these are why 80/20 thinking is unconventional—it advises you to go against the tide. Because of the cyclical nature of the stock market, value investing, when done right, will inevitably lead to big rewards.

All the tips we've suggested so far converge into our next suggestion: invest in stocks that are connected to fields you are a relative expert in. These could be shares relating to the industry you work in, where your hobbies lie, or any particular interest of yours. So, if you like cars, you might want to invest in automobile companies that are trading publicly. Even if you don't feel like an expert in any particular area, it pays to stick to one area and familiarize yourself with that industry rather than diversifying your options.

A list of techniques revolving around using the 80/20 principle effectively would be remiss if it didn't recommend the elimination of underperforming assets, and this applies to investments as well. If the value of any share falls by more than 15% of the price you paid for it, sell that stock immediately. If you wish to buy it later, wait a week to ensure that the price has stopped falling. Many fortunes have been lost to a mistaken sense of loyalty toward particular underperforming stocks. Make sure you avoid that error.

After investing, the most important area where you need to apply the Pareto principle is in relation to your **spending habits, savings,** and **budgeting**. Regarding these, there are two 80/20 rules which will come in very handy for you. First, 80% of your wealth will come from 20% of your efforts with money. Remember, low effort and high value, so in fact only a limited amount of actions will generate your wealth.

Second, living within or below your means on 80% of your total income and saving the remaining 20% will be the key to building your wealth substantially.

We'll start with the second rule first. The idea here is to take everything you spend your money on in a typical month—food, rent, charity, insurance, petrol, personal expenses, etc.—and restrict the overall expenditure to 80% of what your household makes every month. The remaining 20% of your income should be dedicated toward either savings or generating passive income. This can mean you invest a little every month into your retirement fund, put it into the stock market, pay off debts, etc.

Of these, if you have debts, it's absolutely essential for you to meet the minimum payment for every single debt you owe. It is advisable to go about 10-20% above your minimum payment because the longer you owe money the more you lose. If you follow this pattern for a year, you'll end up making one whole extra payment for that year. This can reduce debts like mortgages by several years. Paying a twenty-five-year mortgage using this rule will resolve your debt three years earlier than expected.

While it's important to know what you should be doing to increase your wealth, there are a few very common things people do to cut spending which you *shouldn't* be doing.

The first of these is cutting discretionary spending. This could apply in a variety of ways for you. Maybe you reduce how much you eat out, or skip that movie you've been wanting to watch at the theaters. You might also cut down on some of your media subscriptions. While all of these tactics will save you money, they are unlikely to make any significant difference to your overall financial situation. However, what they will do is prevent you from enjoying the things you like doing. Although it's possible for you to find cheaper ways to do the same things, it's likely that this strategy will only leave you frustrated.

The second option that many opt for is working overtime. Again, many people do this because it does help in some ways. If you can find the overtime hours to work consistently, it might help you in improving your financial situation somewhat. However, overtime isn't a good long-term strategy toward growing your wealth or managing your finances. It also goes against all the principles of sound 80/20 thinking. If you're in need of urgent money due to some debts, this might be a feasible option in the short-term. But as a general rule, working extra is another strategy that requires too much effort and provides too little return to be worth it for any extended period of time.

As you may have noticed, underlying everything we've discussed so far is the 80/20 way of thinking. Be unconventional in your approach toward finances, particularly when it comes to investing. Be reasonably hedonistic in terms of spending and don't cut out expenses for things you enjoy and look forward to. Don't be linear and do the things everyone else is doing, like developing diversified portfolios or working overtime. Lastly, manage your budget and spending habits in ways that are reflective and suited to *you*.

## 80/20 Health and Fitness

When it comes to eating healthy, social media is always abuzz with the latest fads that supposedly guarantee results. From intermittent fasting to Paleo, Keto, going vegan, Atkins, etc., there are a ton of options out there, and none of them keep the 80/20 principle in mind. They demand wholesale changes in your diet and lifestyle, which you might manage in the short term for positive results—but are you willing to be vegan for the rest of your life? It might be a struggle for some.

Healthy eating programs are plagued with an emphasis on short-term results and expending excessive resources in that pursuit, while completely ignoring the long-term. The very phrase "being on a diet" means that at some point you're going to be off it, which discourages actual, meaningful change in your habits. This is where the 80/20 rule becomes so important. It gives you a framework to follow that can actually be sustained for the rest of your life through minimal effort. Remember, we are trying to do less here.

The golden rule you'll want to remember here is that 80% of the calories you consume in a day should come from healthy sources, while the remaining 20% can be expended on foods you enjoy. The key here is to fit the 80% with foods you enjoy as well to minimize the amount of change you need to make to your existing eating habits.

As always, it's important to remember that the numbers don't need to be 80 and 20. In this case, it is much more likely that the ratio will be even more lopsided and inexact. However, this depends primarily on whether your goal is to lose weight or maintain the level you have right now. With the former, you'll want to minimize indulgence, but with the latter you can leave 20% for foods you like eating.

Let's assume you consume an average of around 2000-2200 calories a day. This leaves you with about 400-500 calories to indulge yourself with. However, that number is lower than it seems. You'll likely exhaust it with a bottle of Coke, an energy bar, or a few peanut-butter sandwiches.

As such, it helps to be a little calorie conscious when it comes to what you're eating. Once you familiarize yourself with the basic calorie values of foods you generally eat, this becomes an almost intuitive process that doesn't require any calculation or effort. While calorie counting isn't essential and you can still get by without it, it's definitely advisable.

One common way that people use the 80/20 diet is on a weekly basis, and not daily. This means that throughout the first five days of the week you stick to the 80% healthy foods you're eating, and only allow indulgences on the weekends. That amounts to approximately four meals in a week where you can eat without worrying too much about calories. However, even here, some moderation is key. Don't let yourself slack off too much while indulging your cravings, and try to still get in some nutrients—otherwise you'll feel terrible and risk losing the health gains you've achieved.

Furthermore, pay attention to your portions, regardless of whether you're eating healthy or indulging. Overeating is a huge cause of weight gain, and one you'll want to avoid especially if you're white knuckling through the week. It's imperative that you fill your 80% with foods you like, otherwise you're going to torture yourself for five days a week and end up gaining weight on the weekends. Try including as many fruits, lean proteins, and whole grains as possible. Also, try to cut down on alcohol. Those are simply empty calories that will quickly drive your weight up.

If you find yourself struggling to lose weight with an 80/20 plan, you might want to consider switching to a 90/10 routine. This will reduce your indulgent meals from four a week to just two. This might not be necessary if you're simply looking to maintain your current weight, but more healthy eating is always beneficial if you can manage it.

Lastly, if you can, add some exercise to the mix. This will aid your weight loss efforts significantly, not just because of the burned calories, but due to improved metabolism from increased muscle mass. The 80/20 rule applies here as well, as 20% of exercises lead to 80% of your results. As such, you won't need to spend too much time exercising if you're doing it well, but it's another habit that will go a long way in getting the results you desire.

## 80/20 Organization

Most of the time, we find ourselves in a situation where we have a multiplicity of tasks we need to complete. However, because we only have so much time, we only end up doing a few of those. The tasks we don't finish get put off for the future, and they stay at the back of our minds as we scramble to find the time to do it all. Yet most of these tasks that we've been putting off or meaning to do but just haven't managed to are part of the unnecessary clutter that's polluting our lives. Most of them are not nearly as important as we might have initially thought, and we can likely do away with them without any adverse consequences.

Through the 80/20 principle, you can identify the tasks that matter and are actually important to you while separating the 80% of meaningless clutter that's a constant presence in our lives, but isn't productive or meaningful in any way.

Decluttering your life is where the reflective aspect of 80/20 thinking shines through. Spend some time thinking about what it is you really want to do, and the activities or tasks that you consider important. Are you really going to read all those books on your desk? Do you truly need to complete every single task on your list, or can you delegate some and get away with not doing some of the others? What are the biggest things you're spending a large portion of your time on that aren't aligned with your goals in life?

Be totally honest with yourself, especially since such reflection can often involve tough decisions. If a lot of your clutter has to do with work, ask yourself whether you'd really be at your current job under more ideal circumstances. If you're a student studying for a major you aren't particularly passionate about, think about whether you want these tasks and others similar to them to stay with you for the foreseeable future.

Alternatively, there are also probably things you like doing which use up too much of your time. As we've stressed, there's no need to completely eliminate things you enjoy. But ask yourself if you could spend a little less time watching television? Maybe you could use some of the time you spend scrolling on your phone more productively. If an activity is central to your leisure time, you can probably get away with keeping it intact. However, there are definitely others that can be eliminated or reduced.

This is one of the big advantages of decluttering your life through the Pareto principle: it forces you to make decisions you otherwise would not have considered. This applies to both things you like and those you dislike doing.

So how do you actually go about decluttering your life? One effective way is to take a more methodical approach and create an 80/20 audit sheet. List all the activities you do regularly or need to do, and segregate them based on whether they are consistent with your major goals in life or not. Of course, some tasks won't be extremely important, but you'll have to do them anyway. Keep those, but be ruthless in your selection.

Based on what your audit sheet looks like, you can then start compiling a daily planner that has more tasks related to the 20% most important activities rather than those that simply clutter up your life.

It's likely that at least some of the clutter you want to eliminate or reduce from your life involves things you habitually do. For example, it's possible you're accustomed to playing video games for a certain number of hours every day. Maybe you like consuming alcohol to relax, which renders you indisposed for the rest of the night. Eliminating clutter like this can be hard because of the role it plays in your routine and the urge that overcomes you when you miss it for a few days.

To beat that urge, the thirty-day challenge is a great technique to use. Essentially, what you need to do is write down the habit or task you want to eliminate and note down the date you've started the challenge. Make a column for date of completion and fill it thirty days after you undertook the challenge, and reflect on your progress. Did you manage to cut the habit? Though this technique might sound overly simplistic, the reason it works is because thirty days is usually enough to break a routine. If you stick to your goal and manage to not do that activity for thirty days, its highly likely you won't feel the urge to do it after the month has passed.

Of course, "clutter" is not just our behaviors or habits, but the physical and material untidiness around us. The 80/20 principle can help here, too. Your external surroundings tend to mirror your inner environment. Have a look at the places in your home or office where you spend the most time, and then, consider all the objects you interact with most.

Look at objects and ask whether they add anything to your life, or are merely taking up space. Even worse, could some clutter be actively getting in the way of what's important? Imagine that you spend 80% of your time using or enjoying just 20% of all your worldly possessions, or that just 20% of your things are supplying 80% of your happiness or convenience. Can you identify that 20% and let go of some of the things that contribute nothing?

The last important item to remember is to replace this clutter in your life with not just things that make you happy, but that also help you further your most important goals.

80/20 Your Way to Happy Relationships

When you think of romantic relationships, the two concepts that are probably the furthest from your mind are productivity and efficiency. As such, it might feel slightly counterintuitive to talk of the Pareto principle when it comes to maintaining relations with the people we care about most. However, as we'll discuss, the 80/20 rule has much to offer when it comes to taking a healthy, balanced approach toward your relationships.

When we look for partners, we tend to be overly idealistic. We want the smartest, most beautiful, most emotionally stable, most hard-working, and the most romantic of partners. While such a figure might well exist in our fantasies, no person on earth possesses all of these qualities. Nobody is a complete package, and everyone comes with their own set of flaws that need to be accommodated, including yourself.

This is exactly what the 80/20 rule of dating tells us. According to this, we can reasonably expect 80% of our partner, or 80% of the time we spend with them to be ideal. But we also need to leave a 20% margin for mistakes, faults, and generally undesirable elements that are a part of every relationship. While in other sections we've emphasized that the numbers do not necessarily have to be 80 and 20, this is one area where those two figures are incredibly apt. The reason behind this is that if we consider a number higher than 80, we inevitably expect too much from our relationship. Alternatively, going below 80 might be tolerable, but isn't ideal.

Even if you aren't already in a relationship, you can use this 80/20 rule to think about whether you would be compatible with a particular person or not. Do they possess roughly 80% of the qualities you've wanted in a significant other? Is the remaining 20% something you can see yourself dealing with in healthy ways? You can't find a person who has 100% of what you want. Using the 80/20 approach gives you a balanced way to assess potential partners whom you see a future with.

If you are currently dating someone, ask yourself whether 80% of the time you spend with your partner is enjoyable. Is the remaining 20% tolerable, or is it excruciatingly bad? It's possible to be in a relationship that suffers from extreme highs and lows. Maybe most of the time you spend together is amazing, but when it's bad, it's really bad. How do you decide whether to continue or let go?

One rule of thumb that can help you navigate such a situation is thinking about whether the regrettable 20% endangers you or your core values in any way. Do you fight because your partner does something you find absolutely abhorrent, like stealing or mistreating other people in her life? If yes, it might be time to move on.

While this is one way of conceptualizing the 80/20 rule in dating, there is also an alternative. The previous interpretation is about all the time you spend with your partner, but this one is about the split between time spent on your relationship versus that spent on yourself. Generally, 80% of your time will likely be devoted to activities that are in some way related to your relationship. However, you'll want to keep 20% aside for activities that are solely for you and help you exercise your freedom or independence.

This tactic will prevent you from becoming overly codependent with your partner, and also ensure you're giving yourself enough space away from the relationship to maintain a sense of personal identity. Too much time spent with your partner can leave you feeling resentful, and this approach will help avoid such issues.

If you're still on the fence about the Pareto principle in dating, there are several advantages to implementing this rule that you may not have considered. Besides giving you a realistic way to analyze your future or current relationships and partners, it reminds us of the fact that we are all human. We all make mistakes, but as long as 80% of your time together is spent happily, the mistakes probably don't matter. Due to our bias for negativity, it is often easy to magnify the faults in our relationships and partners while discounting all the good. The 80/20 approach is a constant reminder to situate individual incidents, good or bad, within a larger picture of your relationship's health.

Another advantage of this rule is that it often helps you turn your attention inwards. It makes you question whether you and your actions are allowing your partner to enjoy your relationship 80% of the time. It's only fair for you to meet the same standard you set for others, and this rule can come in handy for that purpose.

You can use this principle in the same way for your platonic friendships as well. You probably have friends whom you consider close to you, but who are actually more trouble than they're worth. Maybe you've stuck with them because you've known them for a while or because you both have the same social circle. But on an individual level, you're not quite sure you like them all that much.

How can you know for sure? Ask yourself if 80% of the time you spend interacting with them is genuinely positive and fulfilling for you. If it is, they're worth keeping, and you might want to communicate and resolve the issues that are part of the 20% time you don't enjoy. However, if you find that they are simply draining your energy and aren't a good friend to you in the ways you consider fitting, it might be worth considering distancing yourself from them.

Another way to use the principle to improve the quality of your friendships is to figure out which friends you hold closest to you. These are the 20% that provide 80% of your happiness derived from friendships. Chances are you'll be able to name these people almost immediately because they hold a special place in your life. These are the people you should prioritize above all else, especially if you're working or have a family of your own. The 20% of time when things can become unpleasant probably plays a role in these special friendships as well, but you can use the Pareto principle to keep yourself grounded and appreciate the good times more.

Now that we've focused on your happiness within relationships, it's finally time to talk about happiness more generally. After all, that is the main outcome toward which all our efforts are dedicated. Every single thing we do is influenced by how happy we believe it will make us.

However, the Pareto principle states that only about 20% of what we do results in

80% of our happiness. This means that 80% of what we do is either making us unhappy or not contributing to our overall well-being in any meaningful way. With this last application of the Pareto principle, we're going to discuss how you can cut out the useless 80% and make the most of the 20% of things you do that are truly making you happy.

Upon reading this, one objection might immediately spring to your mind. Surely, you wonder, happiness is not such a reductive concept that it can be manipulated so easily? What about all the underlying psychological mechanisms behind the things we do and don't do—how do we resolve those?

While it is true that some people are more inclined toward happiness than others, there are strategies everyone can adopt to make themselves *happier*, if not necessarily happy overall. We might not be in total control of our happiness, but we can make the most of the parts we do control, and that's what we'll focus on with this application of the 80/20 principle.

Two major ways we can affect our happiness levels are first, by making ourselves more emotionally intelligent, and second, by modifying the way we think of ourselves. To start with the former, emotional intelligence is our capacity to do things like motivate ourselves, delay gratification, regulate our moods, empathize with ourselves, and not let stress get the better of us. You can probably immediately see why this concept has so much to do with happiness.

So how do you cultivate better emotional intelligence? Identify the circumstances and environments in which you are most positive and most negative. Think of these locations and who you're surrounded by, what you're doing in those circumstances, etc. Try to situate yourself more in the circumstances and environments that inspire positivity. Do things that make you feel in control, try to be more self-aware instead of only looking outwards, and learn to respond well to constructive criticism.

As for changing how you think about yourself, consider this question. Do you think you're a successful or unsuccessful person? If you think you've been unsuccessful, you can rest assured that many have achieved much less than you and have considered themselves a success. But while their perception of success contributes to further success, your impression of failure limits this potential.

Similarly, ask yourself if you are happy or unhappy? The answer to this doesn't just depend on how you've felt in the past, but also on the way you choose to feel in the present and future. If you choose to be happy and perceive yourself as such, psychologists say that this tendency will go a long way in actually making you happy. This can be the first step in cultivating a sense of self-worth. Once you've chosen to be happy, think of all the good things you've ever done and build on your strengths.

You may feel like you're deceiving yourself by putting up this façade of happiness, but in fact the real self-deception lies in having a negative sense of self-worth. This comes back to our negativity bias—we pay more attention to the bad than the good. By instead making a conscious effort to concentrate on the latter, not only will you avoid self-deception, but also increase your happiness levels.

While both of these are long-term processes that take time to fully implement, there are also things you can do right now that will make you happier much sooner. Some of these things are as basic as drinking more water, which has a tremendous impact on your mental well-being. Eating more fruits and vegetables has a similar impact because they make us more alert, improve quality of sleep, prevent gastric issues, etc.

You can also prioritize the 20% of your friendships that provide 80% of the fulfillment you experience. Think and narrow down the handful of people in your life who truly matter, and give them your time and effort. Lastly, fill your life with the 20% experiences that provide 80% of your happiness. Do the things you enjoy doing and which reinforce a sense of purpose in you. Conversely, find the things that make you feel negative emotions and cut them out as far as possible.

Takeaways

- We can apply the Pareto principle not just to business and productivity, but to maximize our own sense of happiness, fulfillment and contentment in life. Here, the principle is more an attitude or approach to living, one that is characterized by a few key features: it's reflexive (i.e. it concerns you and your inner wants and needs), unconventional (i.e. about what actually works, not just what's the unquestioned norm), hedonistic (based on pleasure and happiness) and non-linear (all about thinking outside the box!).
- With personal finances, we can use the principle to maximize our investments, our expenditures and our savings strategies. The constant concern is, which actions yield the most? With investments, this means an unbalanced portfolio and higher

risk stock market investments, since the stock market has a lower barrier to entry but high potential gains. In budgeting, the principle can alert us to those changes that make the biggest difference. We don't need to "sweat the small stuff" if we make a few smart, impactful changes.

- With our health, the principle reminds us that 100% perfection is not necessary—if we stick to a healthy plan most of the time, we can be a little flexible with occasional indulgences or mistakes.

- The 80/20 rule is excellent for decluttering, reminding us that much of what we have in our lives is not nearly as important as we think it is, and can be discarded. We need to be honest about what is actually serving us and get rid of what isn't adding anything, or what is actively harming us.

- In relationships, we can use the principle to forgive ourselves and others for not being 100% perfect, and to understand that if the *most essential* features are in place, we can let smaller flaws slide since we know they won't have a significant impact on our overall relationship success. The rule helps us think about our compatibility with others and our standards in dating—what characteristics are truly essential, and what can we compromise on? In friendship, too, we can learn which of our connections are contributing most to our happiness and structure our time accordingly.

Generally, in every area of our personal lives, the 80/20 principle emphasizes that we need to focus on those things we can change, and let go of what we can't. We can always make large gains by improving our emotional attitude, so our efforts should always be to prioritize our mindset first.

## CHAPTER 1. THE WORLD TURNS 80/20

- According to the 80/20 principle, there are a small set of inputs or factors that make the biggest impact on the total outcome. Roughly 20% of the effort is behind 80% of the results. The numbers can vary widely, with 80 and 20 being just one distribution, and this pattern is observed not just in the business world, but in our personal lives as well.

- This rule was first discovered by the Italian economist Vilfredo Pareto. While observing the distribution of property amongst the Italian population, he found that 20% of Italians own 80% of all private property. He researched this phenomenon further and discovered that this lopsided distribution is prevalent in many other countries as well. Unfortunately, Pareto's ground-breaking discovery was ignored for several decades before others independently observed the same patterns.

- Once the principle was rediscovered, it was adopted by large tech companies like IBM, which used it to improve their computer software. This and similar successes led to the principle's popularization.

- One of the main reasons the 80/20 rule is so important is that it goes against our conventional way of thinking. We tend to assume that the world is a fair place, that things always work out in egalitarian ways, and that one factor is generally as valuable as the next. However, the Pareto principle reverses this belief by saying that only a few elements are truly worth our effort.

- You can see the Pareto principle everywhere around you. Be it dating apps, where large numbers of men are chasing very few women, or sports, where a couple of players determine the team's success, a few causes dominate the end results. By tapping into this potential of the vital few in your own life, you can use the Pareto principle to great effect.

To use the principle in your academic studies, identify only those chapters, concepts, or definitions that help you understand the bulk of the material—e.g. study just the key chemical equations in a chapter first, and spend less effort going over the examples and illustrations.

In your personal life, zoom in on only those activities that most constitute "quality time" with your partner, and always prioritize those. At work, regularly ask what's actually effective and deliberately spend less time doing things like admin or useless process work. The principle even applies when you focus on the only piece of constructive/negative feedback you've received. Using this to inspire your improvements will be so much more effective than considering dozens of complimentary but vague comments.

## CHAPTER 2. THE 80/20 RULE AS A LIFE PRINCIPLE

- Three simple maxims can help us use the 80/20 rule in everyday life: *less is more, always work backwards, and most things don't matter*. Firstly, don't do a lot of busy work simply because it feels like you're making progress—always try to work smarter, not harder simply for the sake of working harder. Secondly, always make sure your goals are crystal clear so you can work backwards and decide which actions matter—and which don't. Finally, understand that some factors simply matter much less than others, and let go of the minor details to focus on the more important ones.
- Use smart questions to zoom in what ultimately matters. Get curious about the *biggest* rewards, costs, obstacles and sources of joy, and don't worry about considering *all* of them.

- The numbers don't have to be in an 80/20 ratio and they don't need to add up to 100. Rather, the 80/20 fraction is simply meant to illustrate that one side of the equation is significantly larger than the opposite.
- Understand that the principle doesn't encourage laziness but optimizes the energy that you do spend, maximizing on its returns. At the same time, don't think that you can completely ignore the 80%--it needs your attention, just relatively less compared to the 20%.
- The effectiveness of the principle depends on your accuracy in identifying the most important 20%. You'll make mistakes in the beginning, but it's a learning curve— constantly check in with your appraisal and adjust as necessary. Gather objective data to analyze so you can make objective, rational decisions as much as possible.
- You can use the Pareto principle in your career, specifically your job search. Expend the least energy for

the most reward by honing in on only those job roles most appropriate for you early on. This means you search less, and come up with fewer hits—but those hits will be of greater quality, saving you time and energy.

- You can use the Pareto principle in your business, too, by letting it guide your marketing efforts. Using gathered analytics data, for instance, you can identify the top performing posts, campaigns or keywords, so you can focus on those.

Though it's true that the principle isn't a magic formula that will solve all your problems (or save you from having to consider the 80%), it can be an enormous time and energy saver if used correctly. In short, the 80/20 principle is about using data or observations to help identify and optimize on the most essential aspects of any process, so that you spend the least energy for the most gain. A simple example is a company offering free samples at a convention. Using data, they can identify their top performing and most popular item and promote that exclusively, knowing that this move is likely to generate more revenue than any other.

## CHAPTER 3. THE LESS IS MORE FRAMEWORK

- There are three useful steps to follow in implementing the 80/20 rule for maximum effect. First, identify your goals by writing down a list, but selecting only the two or three most important ones—these are the ones that inspire passion and productivity, and align with your values and life purpose. These are the goals that have the highest chance of creating happiness, although it's wise to regularly check in with your values, as they can change with time.
- The next step is to identify the 80/20 you'll take. Look at your chosen goals and categorize them as either low effort, low reward (filler tasks), high effort, high reward (big projects), high effort, low reward (hard slogs), or low effort, high reward (quick wins, or the 80/20 path that you want to take first). Once you've

decided which path is easiest and most rewarding, you can prioritize your actions accordingly.

- The third step is to identify these tasks and actions. You can get an idea of useful tasks by looking to other successful people, but beware: you may find success doing the exact opposite! Once you've identified useful actions, make as many of them habitual/automatic as possible by building them into routines.
- These three steps can apply to any area of life, such as relationships, habits, business or study, health and miscellaneous activities. By choosing the most important goal, and identifying the most effective and elegant way to achieve that objective, you are essentially outlining the swiftest path to the outcome that will give you the most satisfaction and reward, no matter what area of life you apply the method to.

In relationships, for example, you can focus your attentions on that small handful of people who genuinely bring the most happiness to your life, and similarly, you can look at your daily habits and ask honestly what daily actions are really bringing you closer to happiness and success, and which aren't. Where hobbies are concerned, you can frequently examine your activities and ask where the best 20% of your experience actually comes from, and with your health you can identify and eliminate your single worst habit, or build on your most effective one.

## CHAPTER 4. THE 80/20 OF PROFESSIONAL SUCCESS

- In business, the 80/20 model works because it closely mirrors the way the market itself behaves. Using the 80/20 principle can lead to compounding efficiencies that quickly cause the business to represent the 20% most successful businesses.
- The principle applies to decision making, and cuts short "analysis paralysis" or time wasted on deliberation over the unimportant

80%. Instead, it's wise to act sooner and get feedback quickly, so as to course correct as soon as possible. In project management, the principle can help to slice away at useless organizational complexity, for example by identifying only those actions that lead to a single high-value goal. With employees, the principle helps you identify the top performers so they can be supported, and by the same token pinpoint inefficiencies and waste, so that costs can be cut, and the biggest inefficiency culprits found and eliminated.

- The principle can help you appraise the functioning of your business in areas such as products (categorize each according to their profitability), customers (identify those who purchase a lot but cost a little to maintain, and downplay the reverse), splits (such as the proportion of old vs. new clients, big vs. small jobs, etc.), and competition (asking who they are and how they compare to you can help you adjust your strategy accordingly).

- For employees, the 80/20 rules can help shape time-management efforts, but goes a step further and inspires "time revolution"—rethinking time entirely, and undoing the assumption that effort is always proportional to outcome. This means delegation without guilt, using time wisely and not just being productive, and frequently identifying high and low-value tasks for yourself. It also means seeking feedback often and early so you can adjust sooner rather than later, after you've already wasted time on unimportant tasks.

The way you choose to use the Pareto Principle in your own business or as an employee will depend greatly on the business, your role in it and your ultimate goals. Nevertheless, the 80/20 principle can improve almost every business or work decision, from your content marketing or SEO strategy to the way in which you identify and reward top performers, to your leadership approach in general.

## CHAPTER 5. 80/20 FOR A BETTER YOU

- We can apply the Pareto principle not just to business and productivity, but to maximize our own sense of happiness, fulfillment and contentment in life. Here, the principle is more an attitude or approach to living, one that is characterized by a few key features: it's reflexive (i.e. it concerns you and your inner wants and needs), unconventional (i.e. about what actually works, not just what's the unquestioned norm), hedonistic (based on pleasure and happiness) and non-linear (all about thinking outside the box!).

- With personal finances, we can use the principle to maximize our investments, our expenditures and our savings strategies. The constant concern is, which actions yield the most? With investments, this means an unbalanced portfolio and higher risk stock market investments, since the stock market has a lower barrier to entry but high potential gains. In budgeting, the principle can alert us to those changes that make the biggest difference. We don't need to "sweat the small stuff" if we make a few smart, impactful changes.

- With our health, the principle reminds us that 100% perfection is not necessary—if we stick to a healthy plan most of the time, we can be a little flexible with occasional indulgences or mistakes.
- The 80/20 rule is excellent for decluttering, reminding us that much of what we have in our lives is not nearly as important as we think it is, and can be discarded. We need to be honest about what is actually serving us and get rid of what isn't adding anything, or what is actively harming us.
- In relationships, we can use the principle to forgive ourselves and others for not being 100% perfect, and to understand that if the *most essential* features are in place, we can

let smaller flaws slide since we know they won't have a significant impact on our overall relationship success. The rule helps us think about our compatibility with others and our standards in dating—what characteristics are truly essential, and what can we compromise on? In friendship, too, we can learn which of our connections are contributing most to our happiness and structure our time accordingly.

Generally, in every area of our personal lives, the 80/20 principle emphasizes that we need to focus on those things we can change, and let go of what we can't. We can always make large gains by improving our emotional attitude, so our efforts should always be to prioritize our mindset first.